TOGAF® VERSION 9 – A POCKET GUIDE

D0810837

About the TOGAF® series

The TOGAF® series contains the official publications on TOGAF on behalf of The Open Group, including:

- TOGAF® Version 9
- TOGAF® Version 9 – A Pocket Guide
- TOGAF® 9 Foundation Study Guide
- TOGAF® 9 Certified Study Guide

For the latest information on TOGAF® visit www.opengroup.org/togaf

Other publications by Van Haren Publishing

Van Haren Publishing specializes in titles on Best Practices, methods and standards within IT and business management.

These publications are grouped in the following series: ITSM Library, Best Practice and IT Management Topics. Van Haren Publishing is also publisher on behalf of ITSMF, ASL BiSL Foundation, IPMA Nederland, PMI Netherlands Chapter and Platform Outsourcing Nederland.

For the latest information visit www.vanharen.net

TOGAF® Version 9

A POCKET GUIDE

Title: TOGAF® Version 9 – A Pocket Guide
A publication of: The Open Group
Authors: Andrew Josey, The Open Group
                      Professor Rachel Harrison, Stratton Edge Consulting
                      Paul Homan, IBM
                      Matthew F. Rouse, EDS
                      Tom van Sante, Getronics
                      Mike Turner, Capgemini
                      Paul van der Merwe, Real IRM
Publisher: Van Haren Publishing, Zaltbommel, www.vanharen.net

ISBN: 978 90 8753 232 1

Edition: 2nd edition, 1st impression, January 2009
                      2nd edition, 2nd impression, June 2009
                      2nd edition, 3rd impression, December 2009
                      2nd edition, 4th impression, August 2010
                      2nd edition, 5th impression, March 2011

Layout and Cover design: CO2 Premedia, Amersfoort-NL

Print: Wilco, Amersfoort – NL

Copyright: © 2008, The Open Group

In the event of any discrepancy between text in this document and the official TOGAF
9 documentation, the TOGAF 9 documentation remains the authoritative version
for certification, testing by examination, and other purposes. The official TOGAF 9
documentation can be obtained online at www.opengroup.org/togaf.

Document Number: G092

Published by The Open Group, January 2009

Comments relating to the material contained in this document may be submitted to:

The Open Group
Apex Plaza, Forbury Road
Reading
Berkshire RG1 1AX
United Kingdom

or by electronic mail to:
ogspecs@opengroup.org

Contents

Preface

This Document

This Pocket Guide is based on TOGAF® Version 9 Enterprise Edition. It is intended to help architects focus on the efficient and effective operations of their organization and senior managers understand the basics of the TOGAF framework for enterprise architecture. It is organized as follows:

- Chapter 1 provides a high-level view of TOGAF, enterprise architecture, and the contents and key concepts of TOGAF.
- Chapter 2 provides an introduction to the Architecture Development Method (ADM), the method that TOGAF provides to develop enterprise architectures.
- Chapter 3 provides an overview of key techniques and deliverables of the ADM cycle.
- Chapter 4 provides an overview of the guidelines for adapting the ADM.
- Chapter 5 provides an introduction to the Architecture Content Framework, a structured metamodel for architectural artifacts.
- Chapter 6 provides an introduction to the Enterprise Continuum, a high-level concept that can be used with the ADM to develop an enterprise architecture.
- Chapter 7 provides an introduction to the TOGAF Reference Models, including the TOGAF Foundation Architecture and the Integrated Information Infrastructure Reference Model (III-RM).
- Chapter 8 provides an introduction to the Architecture Capability Framework, a set of resources provided for establishment and operation of an architecture function within an enterprise.
- Appendix A provides an overview of the differences between TOGAF 9 and TOGAF 8.1.1.

The audience for this document is:

- Enterprise architects, business architects, IT architects, data architects, systems architects, solutions architects, and senior managers seeking a first introduction to TOGAF

A prior knowledge of enterprise architecture is not required. After reading this document, the reader seeking further information should refer to the TOGAF 9 documentation[1] available online at www.opengroup.org/architecture/togaf9-doc/arch and also available as TOGAF 9 "The Book".

About TOGAF Version 9

TOGAF 9 provides a wide-ranging set of revisions to the TOGAF specification to improve the value of the TOGAF framework: It has been designed as an evolution from TOGAF 8.1.1, adding further detail and clarification to what is already proven. Major new features of TOGAF 9 include:

Modular Structure: TOGAF 9 introduces a modular structure. Content that was contained within the TOGAF 8.1.1 Resource Base has been classified and moved into parts that have a defined purpose (as opposed to generic "resources"). The modular structure supports:

- Greater usability – defined purpose for each part; can be used in isolation as a standalone set of guidelines
- Incremental adoption of the TOGAF specification

Content Framework: TOGAF 9 includes a content framework to drive greater consistency in the outputs that are created when following the Architecture Development Method (ADM). The TOGAF content framework provides a detailed model of architectural work products.

---

1 The Open Group Architecture Framework (TOGAF), Version 9 Enterprise Edition (ISBN: 978-90-8753-094-5, G091v); refer to www.opengroup.org/bookstore/catalog/g091.htm

Extended Guidance: TOGAF 9 features an extended set of concepts and guidelines to support the establishment of an integrated hierarchy of architectures being developed by teams within larger organizations that operate within an overarching architectural governance model. In particular, the following concepts are introduced:

- Partitioning: A number of different techniques and considerations on how to partition the various architectures within an enterprise.
- Architecture Repository: A logical information model for an Architecture Repository which can be used as an integrated store for all outputs created by executing the ADM.
- Capability Framework: A more structured definition of the organization, skills, roles, and responsibilities required to operate an effective enterprise architecture capability. The new TOGAF materials also provide guidance on a process that can be followed to identify and establish an appropriate architecture capability.

Architectural Styles: TOGAF 9, in its new Part III: ADM Guidelines & Techniques, brings together a set of supporting materials that show in detail how the ADM can be applied to specific situations:

- The varying uses of iteration that are possible within the ADM and when each technique should be applied
- The linkages between the TOGAF ADM and Service Oriented Architecture (SOA)
- The specific considerations required to address security architecture within the ADM
- The various types of architecture development required within an enterprise and how these relate to one another

Additional ADM Detail: TOGAF 9 includes additional detailed information supporting the execution of the ADM. Particular areas of enhancement are:

- The Preliminary phase features extended guidance on establishing an enterprise architecture framework and planning for architecture development.
- The Opportunities & Solutions and Migration Planning phases feature a more detailed and robust method for defining and planning enterprise transformation, based on the principles of capability-based planning.

Conventions Used in this Document

The following conventions are used throughout this document in order to help identify important information and avoid confusion over the intended meaning:

- Ellipsis (…)
  Indicates a continuation; such as an incomplete list of example items, or a continuation from preceding text.
- **Bold**
  Used to highlight specific terms.
- *Italics*
  Used for emphasis. May also refer to other external documents.

About The Open Group

The Open Group is a vendor-neutral and technology-neutral consortium, whose vision of Boundaryless Information Flow™ will enable access to integrated information within and between enterprises based on open standards and global interoperability. The Open Group works with customers, suppliers, consortia, and other standards bodies. Its role is to capture, understand, and address current and emerging requirements, establish policies, and share best practices; to facilitate interoperability, develop consensus, and evolve and integrate specifications and Open Source technologies; to offer a comprehensive set of services to enhance the operational efficiency of consortia; and to operate the industry's premier certification service.

Further information on The Open Group is available at www.opengroup.org.

The Open Group has over 15 years' experience in developing and operating certification programs and has extensive experience developing and facilitating industry adoption of test suites used to validate conformance to an open standard or specification.

The Open Group publishes a wide range of technical documentation, the main part of which is focused on development of Technical and Product Standards and Guides, but which also includes White Papers, Technical Studies, and Business Titles.

A catalog is available at www.opengroup.org/bookstore.

Trademarks

About the Authors

Andrew Josey, The Open Group

Andrew Josey is Director of Standards within The Open Group. He is currently managing the standards process for The Open Group, and has recently led the standards development projects for TOGAF 9, IEEE Std 1003.1-2008 (POSIX), and the core specifications of the Single UNIX Specification, Version 4. Previously, he has led the development and operation of many of The Open Group's certification development projects, including industry-wide certification programs for the UNIX system, the Linux Standard Base, TOGAF, and IEEE POSIX. He is a member of the IEEE, USENIX, UKUUG, and the Association of Open Group Enterprise Architects.

Professor Rachel Harrison, Stratton Edge Consulting

Rachel Harrison is a Visiting Professor of Computer Science at the University of Reading and Director of Stratton Edge Consulting. Formerly she was Professor of Computer Science, Head of the Department of Computer Science, and Director of Research for the School of System Engineering at the University of Reading. She obtained an MA in Mathematics from Oxford University, an MSc in Computer Science from UCL, and a PhD in Computer Science from the University of Southampton. Current research interests include enterprise architecture, systems' evolution, software metrics, requirements engineering, and process modeling. Her consultancy services include preparation of the TOGAF Study Guide and its accompanying training course materials for The Open Group. Professor Harrison is a member of the IEEE Computer Society, the ACM, the BCS, and is also a Chartered Engineer.

Paul Homan, IBM

Paul Homan is a Technology Strategy Consultant within IBM's Global Business Services. He is a Certified Master IT Architect, specializing in enterprise architecture with over 20 years' experience in IT. Highly passionate and practically experienced in architecture, strategy, design authority, and governance areas, Paul is particularly interested in enterprise architecture leadership, requirements management, and business architecture. He joined IBM from end-user environments, having worked as Chief Architect in both the UK Post Office and Royal Mail. He has not only established enterprise architecture practices, but has also lived with the results!

Matthew F. Rouse, EDS

Matthew Rouse is a member of the EDS Global Architecture Capability. Matthew has over 20 years' IS/IT experience in applications development, system architecture, IS/IT strategy, and enterprise architecture. He brings expertise in strategic IS/IT planning and architecture to ensure that enterprises align their IS/IT investments with their business objectives. Matthew is a Chartered IT Professional member of the British Computer Society, a Master Certified IT Architect, and a member of the IEEE Computer Society.

Tom van Sante, Getronics

Tom van Sante is Principal Consultant for Getronics. He started his career in IT over 25 years ago after studying architecture at the Technical University in Delft. Working in a variety of functions, from operations to management, he has always operated on the borders between business and IT. He was involved in the introduction and development of ITIL/ASL/BiSL in the Netherlands. Tom van Sante has worked in numerous appointments for the EU and Dutch ministries advising on the use of IT in modern society. He is currently responsible for the introduction and development of TOGAF within Getronics.

Mike Turner, Capgemini

Mike Turner is an Enterprise Architect at Capgemini and has been focusing exclusively on enterprise architecture for the past six years. Mike spends his time helping organizations to grow enterprise architecture capabilities and assisting organizations in the realization of strategic change through the use of enterprise architecture. Mike has a deep understanding of enterprise architecture frameworks, leading Capgemini's development effort on TOGAF Version 9 and also working in the core team that developed the SAP Enterprise Architecture Framework (a joint initiative between Capgemini and SAP).

Paul van der Merwe, Real IRM

Paul van der Merwe, Consulting & Training Manager at Real IRM, is one of South Africa's most dynamic and insightful enterprise architecture practitioners. A conceptual thinker, he has driven a number of advances in the fields in which he has specialized, among them software development, business intelligence, and enterprise architecture. He presented the first TOGAF certification course in South Africa. He frequently presents on enterprise architecture, the Zachman Framework, and governance, and has trained in these disciplines on three continents. Paul is also a respected academic who presents a post-graduate course in the Department of Informatics at the University of Pretoria.

Acknowledgements

The Open Group gratefully acknowledges the following:

- Past and present members of The Open Group Architecture Forum for developing TOGAF.
- Capgemini and SAP for contributed materials
- The following reviewers of this document:
  - Bill Estrem
  - Henry Franken
  - Judith Jones
  - Henk Jonkers
  - Kiichiro Onishi
  - Roger Reading
  - Saverio Rinaldi
  - Robert Weisman
  - Nicholas Yakoubovsky

Chapter 1
Introduction to TOGAF®

This chapter provides an introduction to TOGAF 9.

Topics addressed in this chapter include:

- An Introduction to TOGAF
- TOGAF, its structure and content
- The kinds of architecture that TOGAF addresses

1.1 Introduction to TOGAF 9

TOGAF is an architecture framework – **The Open Group Architecture Framework**. Put simply, TOGAF is a tool for assisting in the acceptance, production, use, and maintenance of architectures. It is based on an iterative process model supported by best practices and a re-usable set of existing architectural assets.

TOGAF is developed and maintained by The Open Group Architecture Forum. The first version of TOGAF, developed in 1995, was based on the US Department of Defense Technical Architecture Framework for Information Management (TAFIM). Starting from this sound foundation, The Open Group Architecture Forum has developed successive versions of TOGAF at regular intervals and published each one on The Open Group public web site.

This document covers TOGAF Version 9, referred to as "TOGAF 9" within the text of this document. TOGAF 9 was first published in January 2009. TOGAF 9 is an evolution from TOGAF 8.1.1 and a description of the changes is provided in Appendix A.

TOGAF 9 can be used for developing a broad range of different enterprise architectures. TOGAF complements, and can be used in conjunction with, other frameworks that are more focused on specific deliverables for particular vertical sectors such as Government, Telecommunications, Manufacturing, Defense, and Finance. The key to TOGAF is the method – the TOGAF Architecture Development Method (ADM) – for developing an enterprise architecture that addresses business needs.

1.2   Structure of the TOGAF Document

The TOGAF 9 document is divided into seven parts, as summarized in Table 1.

Table 1: Structure of the TOGAF Document

Part I: Introduction	This part provides a high-level introduction to the key concepts of enterprise architecture and, in particular, to the TOGAF approach. It contains the definitions of terms used throughout TOGAF and release notes detailing the changes between this version and the previous version of TOGAF.
Part II: Architecture Development Method	This part is the core of TOGAF. It describes the TOGAF Architecture Development Method (ADM) – a step-by-step approach to developing an enterprise architecture.
Part III: ADM Guidelines and Techniques	This part contains a collection of guidelines and techniques available for use in applying the ADM.
Part IV: Architecture Content Framework	This part describes the TOGAF content framework, including a structured metamodel for architectural artifacts, the use of re-usable Architecture Building Blocks (ABBs), and an overview of typical architecture deliverables.
Part V: Enterprise Continuum and Tools	This part discusses appropriate taxonomies and tools to categorize and store the outputs of architecture activity within an enterprise.
Part VI: TOGAF Reference Models	This part provides two architectural reference models, namely the TOGAF Technical Reference Model (TRM), and the Integrated Information Infrastructure Reference Model (III-RM).
Part VII: Architecture Capability Framework	This part discusses the organization, processes, skills, roles, and responsibilities required to establish and operate an architecture practice within an enterprise.

1.3 What is Architecture in the Context of TOGAF?

ISO/IEC 42010:2007[2] defines "architecture" as:

"The fundamental organization of a system, embodied in its components, their relationships to each other and the environment, and the principles governing its design and evolution."

TOGAF embraces and extends this definition. In TOGAF, "architecture" has two meanings depending upon the context:

1. A formal description of a system, or a detailed plan of the system at a component level to guide its implementation
2. The structure of components, their inter-relationships, and the principles and guidelines governing their design and evolution over time

1.4 What kinds of Architecture does TOGAF deal with?

TOGAF 9 covers the development of four related types of architecture. These four types of architecture are commonly accepted as subsets of an overall enterprise architecture, all of which TOGAF is designed to support. They are shown in Table 2.

Table 2: Architecture Types Supported by TOGAF

Architecture Type	Description
Business Architecture	The business strategy, governance, organization, and key business processes.
Data Architecture[3]	The structure of an organization's logical and physical data assets and data management resources.
Application Architecture	A blueprint for the individual application systems to be deployed, their interactions, and their relationships to the core business processes of the organization.

---

2 ISO/IEC 42010:2007, Systems and Software Engineering – Recommended Practice for Architectural Description of Software-Intensive Systems, Edition 1 (technically identical to ANSI/IEEE Std 1471-2000).

3 Data Architecture is called Information Architecture in some organizations.

Architecture Type	Description
Technology Architecture	The logical software and hardware capabilities that are required to support the deployment of business, data, and application services. This includes IT infrastructure, middleware, networks, communications, processing, and standards.

1.5   What does TOGAF Contain?

TOGAF reflects the structure and content of an architecture capability within an enterprise, as shown in Figure 1.

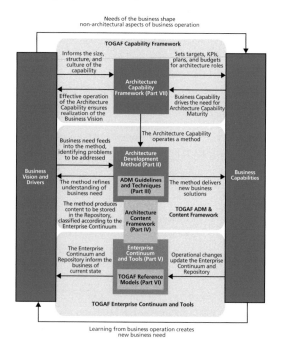

Figure 1: TOGAF Content Overview

Central to TOGAF is the Architecture Development Method (documented in TOGAF 9, Part II). The architecture capability (documented in TOGAF 9, Part VII) operates the method. The method is supported by a number of guidelines and techniques (documented in TOGAF 9, Part III). This produces content to be stored in the repository (documented in TOGAF 9, Part IV), which is classified according to the Enterprise Continuum (documented in TOGAF 9, Part V). The repository is initially populated with the TOGAF Reference Models (documented in TOGAF 9, Part VI).

1.5.1 The Architecture Development Method (ADM)

The **ADM** describes how to derive an organization-specific enterprise architecture that addresses business requirements. The ADM is the major component of TOGAF and provides guidance for architects on a number of levels:

- It provides a number of **architecture development phases** (Business Architecture, Information Systems Architectures, Technology Architecture) in a cycle, as an overall process template for architecture development activity.
- It provides a **narrative of each architecture phase**, describing the phase in terms of objectives, approach, inputs, steps, and outputs. The inputs and outputs sections provide a definition of the architecture content structure and deliverables (a detailed description of the phase inputs and phase outputs is given in the Architecture Content Framework).
- It provides cross-phase summaries that cover requirements management.

The ADM is described further in Chapter 2.

1.5.2 ADM Guidelines and Techniques

ADM Guidelines and Techniques provides a number of guidelines and techniques to support the application of the ADM. The guidelines address adapting the ADM to deal with a number of usage scenarios, including different process styles (e.g., the use of iteration) and also specific specialty architectures (such as security). The techniques support specific tasks within the ADM (such as defining principles, business scenarios, gap analysis, migration planning, risk management, etc.)

ADM Guidelines are described further in Chapter 4. ADM Techniques are described in detail in Chapter 3, together with key deliverables.

1.5.3 Architecture Content Framework

The **Architecture Content Framework** provides a detailed model of architectural work products, including deliverables, artifacts within deliverables, and the Architecture Building Blocks (ABBs) that deliverables represent.

The Architecture Content Framework is described further in Chapter 5.

1.5.4 The Enterprise Continuum

The **Enterprise Continuum** provides a model for structuring a virtual repository and provides methods for classifying architecture and solution artifacts, showing how the different types of artifacts evolve, and how they can be leveraged and re-used. This is based on architectures and solutions (models, patterns, architecture descriptions, etc.) that exist within the enterprise and in the industry at large, and which the enterprise has collected for use in the development of its architectures.

The Enterprise Continuum is described further in Chapter 6.

1.5.5 TOGAF Reference Models

TOGAF provides two reference models for possible inclusion in an enterprise's own Enterprise Continuum, namely the TOGAF **Technical**

Reference Model (TRM) and the **Integrated Information Infrastructure Model** (III-RM).

The TOGAF Reference Models are described further in Chapter 7.

1.5.6 The Architecture Capability Framework

The **Architecture Capability Framework** is a set of resources, guidelines, templates, background information, etc. provided to help the architect establish an architecture practice within an organization.

The Architecture Capability Framework is described further in Chapter 8.

Chapter 2
The Architecture Development Method

This chapter describes the Architecture Development Method (ADM), its relationship to the rest of TOGAF, and high-level considerations for its use. It also includes a summary of each phase within the ADM.

Topics addressed in this chapter include:
- An introduction to the ADM
- The phases of the ADM
- The objectives, steps, inputs, and outputs to the ADM phases
- Requirements Management during the ADM cycle
- Scoping the architecture activity

2.1 What is the ADM?

The ADM, a result of contributions from many architects, forms the core of TOGAF. It is a method for deriving organization-specific enterprise architectures and is specifically designed to address business requirements. The ADM describes:
- A reliable, proven way of developing and using an enterprise architecture
- A method of developing architectures on different levels[4] (business, application, data, technology) that enable the architect to ensure that a complex set of requirements are adequately addressed
- Guidelines on tools for architecture development

---

4 In TOGAF this is termed as a set of architecture domains.

2.2   What are the Phases of the ADM?

The ADM consists of a number of phases that cycle through a range of architecture domains that enable the architect to ensure that a complex set of requirements is adequately addressed. The basic structure of the ADM is shown in Figure 2.

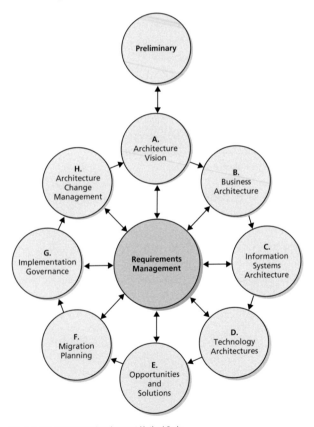

Figure 2: The Architecture Development Method Cycle

The ADM is applied iteratively throughout the entire process, between phases, and within them. Throughout the ADM cycle, there should be frequent validation of results against the original requirements, both those for the whole ADM cycle, and those for the particular phase of the process. Such validation should reconsider scope, detail, schedules, and milestones. Each phase should consider assets produced from previous iterations of the process and external assets from the marketplace, such as other frameworks or models.

The ADM supports the concept of iteration at three levels:
- **Cycling around the ADM**: The ADM is presented in a circular manner indicating that the completion of one phase of architecture work directly feeds into subsequent phases of architecture work.
- **Iterating between phases**: TOGAF describes the concept of iterating across phases (e.g., returning to Business Architecture on completion of Technology Architecture).
- **Cycling around a single phase**: TOGAF supports repeated execution of the activities within a single ADM phase as a technique for elaborating architectural content.

Further information on iteration is given in TOGAF 9, Part III: ADM Guidelines and Techniques (see Chapter 4).

Table 3: Architecture Development Method Activities by Phase

ADM Phase	Activity
Preliminary	Prepare the organization for successful TOGAF architecture projects. Undertake the preparation and initiation activities required to meet the business directive for a new enterprise architecture, including the definition of an organization-specific architecture framework and tools, and the definition of principles.
Requirements Management	Every stage of a TOGAF project is based on and validates business requirements. Requirements are identified, stored, and fed into and out of the relevant ADM phases, which dispose of, address, and prioritize requirements.

ADM Phase	Activity
A. Architecture Vision	Set the scope, constraints, and expectations for a TOGAF project. Create the Architecture Vision. Define stakeholders. Validate the business context and create the Statement of Architecture Work. Obtain approvals.
B. Business Architecture **C.** Information Systems Architectures **D.** Technology Architecture	Develop architectures at three levels: Business Information Systems Technology In each case, develop the Baseline and Target Architecture and analyze gaps.
E. Opportunities and Solutions	Perform initial implementation planning and the identification of delivery vehicles for the building blocks identified in the previous phases. Identify major implementation projects, and group them into Transition Architectures.
F. Migration Planning	Analyze cost benefits and risk. Develop detailed Implementation and Migration Plan.
G. Implementation Governance	Provide architectural oversight for the implementation. Prepare and issue Architecture Contracts (Implementation Governance Board). Ensure that the implementation project conforms to the architecture.
H. Architecture Change Management	Provide continual monitoring and a change management process to ensure that the architecture responds to the needs of the enterprise and maximizes the value of the architecture to the business.

2.3   The ADM in Detail

The following tables summarize the objectives, steps, and the inputs and outputs[5] of each phase of the ADM cycle.

---

5   Version numbers for specific deliverables have been omitted from this Pocket Guide since TOGAF states that the ADM numbering scheme is an example and that it should be adapted as appropriate.

2.3.1 Preliminary Phase

The Preliminary phase prepares an organization to undertake successful enterprise architecture projects.

An overview of the phase is given below:

Objectives	Steps
To review the organizational context for conducting enterprise architecture	Scope the enterprise organizations impacted
To identify the stakeholders, their requirements, and priorities	Confirm governance and support frameworks
To confirm the commitment of the stakeholders	Define and establish enterprise architecture team and organization
To identify and scope the elements of the enterprise organizations affected and define the constraints and assumptions; this is particularly important for large organizations where there may be a federated architecture environment	Identify and establish architecture principles
	Select and tailor architecture framework(s)
To define an organization's "architecture footprint"; that is, the people responsible for performing the architecture work, where they are located, and their responsibilities	Implement architecture tools
To define the framework and detailed methodologies that are going to be used to develop the enterprise architecture in the organization; this is typically an adaptation of the ADM	
To set up a governance and support framework to provide business process and architecture governance through the ADM cycle; these will confirm the fitness-for-purpose and ongoing effectiveness of the Target Architecture; normally this includes an initial pilot project	
To select and implement supporting tools and other infrastructure to support the architecture activity	
To define the constraining architecture principles	

Inputs	Outputs
TOGAF	Organizational model for
Other architecture framework(s)	enterprise architecture
Business principles, business goals, and business	Tailored Architecture
drivers	Framework, including
Architecture governance strategy	architecture principles
IT strategy	Initial Architecture Repository
Existing organizational model for enterprise	Restatement of, or reference to,
architecture	business principles, business
Existing architecture framework, if any	goals, and business drivers
Existing architecture principles, if any	Request for Architecture Work
Existing Architecture Repository, if any	Governance Framework

2.3.2 Phase A: Architecture Vision

Phase A is about project establishment and initiates an iteration of
the architecture development cycle, setting the scope, constraints, and
expectations for the iteration. It is required in order to validate the business
context and to create the approved Statement of Architecture Work.

Objectives	Steps
Obtain management commitment for this particular cycle of the ADM	Establish the architecture project
Define and organize an architecture development cycle	Identify stakeholders, concerns, and business requirements
Validate business principles, goals, drivers, and key performance indicators (KPIs)	Confirm and elaborate business goals, business drivers, and constraints
Define, scope, and prioritize architecture tasks	Evaluate business capabilities
Identify stakeholders, their concerns, and objectives	Assess readiness for business transformation
Define business requirements and constraints	Define scope
Articulate an Architecture Vision and value proposition to respond to the requirements and constraints	Confirm and elaborate architecture principles, including business principles
	Develop Architecture Vision
Create a comprehensive plan in line with the project management frameworks adopted by the enterprise	Define the Target Architecture value propositions and KPIs
	Identify the business transformation risks and mitigation activities
Obtain formal approval to proceed	Develop enterprise architecture plans
Understand the impact on, and of, other parallel architecture development cycles	and Statement of Architecture Work; secure approval

Inputs	Outputs
Request for Architecture Work	Approved Statement of Architecture Work
Business principles, business goals, and business drivers	Refined statements of business principles, business goals, and business drivers
Organization model for enterprise architecture	Architecture principles
	Capability assessment
Tailored Architecture Framework, including architecture principles	Tailored Architecture Framework
	Architecture Vision, including:
Populated Architecture Repository; that is, existing architecture documentation (framework description, architecture descriptions, existing baseline descriptions, etc.)	– Refined key high-level stakeholder requirements
	– Baseline Business Architecture (vision)
	– Baseline Data Architecture (vision)
	– Baseline Application Architecture (vision)
	– Baseline Technology Architecture (vision)
	– Target Business Architecture (vision)
	– Target Data Architecture (vision)
	– Target Application Architecture (vision)
	– Target Technology Architecture (vision)
	Communications Plan
	Additional content populating the Architecture Repository

2.3.3 Phase B: Business Architecture

Phase B is about development of a Business Architecture to support an agreed Architecture Vision.

Objectives	Steps
Describe the Baseline Business Architecture	Select reference models, viewpoints, and tools
Develop a Target Business Architecture	Develop Baseline Business Architecture Description
Analyze the gaps between the Baseline and Target Architectures	Develop Target Business Architecture Description
Select architecture viewpoints to demonstrate how stakeholder concerns are addressed in the Business Architecture	Perform gap analysis
	Define roadmap components
	Resolve impacts across the Architecture Landscape
Select tools and techniques for viewpoints	Conduct formal stakeholder review
	Finalize the Business Architecture
	Create Architecture Definition Document

Inputs	Outputs
Request for Architecture Work	Statement of Architecture Work, updated if necessary
Business principles, business goals, and business drivers	Validated business principles, business goals, and business drivers
Capability Assessment	Elaborated Business Architecture principles
Communications Plan	Draft Architecture Definition Document containing content updates:
Organization model for enterprise architecture	
Tailored Architecture Framework	– Baseline Business Architecture (detailed), if appropriate
Approved Statement of Architecture Work	– Target Business Architecture (detailed)
Architecture principles, including business principles, when pre-existing	– Views corresponding to selected viewpoints addressing key stakeholder concerns
Enterprise Continuum	
Architecture Repository	Draft Architecture Requirements Specification including content updates:
Architecture Vision, including:	
– Refined key high-level stakeholder requirements	– Gap analysis results
– Baseline Business Architecture (vision)	– Technical requirements
– Baseline Data Architecture (vision)	– Updated business requirements
– Baseline Application Architecture (vision)	Business Architecture components of an Architecture Roadmap
– Baseline Technology Architecture (vision)	
– Target Business Architecture (vision)	
– Target Data Architecture (vision)	
– Target Application Architecture (vision)	
– Target Technology Architecture (vision)	

2.3.4 Phase C: Information Systems Architectures

Phase C is about documenting the fundamental organization of an organization's IT systems, embodied in the major types of information and the application systems that process them. There are two steps in this phase, which may be developed either sequentially or concurrently:

• Data Architecture

• Application Architecture

2.3.4.1 Data Architecture

Objectives	Steps
Define the types and sources of data needed to support the business, in a way that can be understood by the stakeholders	Select reference models, viewpoints, and tools
	Develop Baseline Data Architecture Description
	Develop Target Data Architecture Description
	Perform gap analysis
	Define roadmap components
	Resolve impacts across the Architecture Landscape
	Conduct formal stakeholder review
	Finalize the Data Architecture
	Create Architecture Definition Document

Inputs	Outputs
Request for Architecture Work	Statement of Architecture Work, updated if necessary
Capability Assessment	Validated data principles, or new data principles
Communications Plan	Draft Architecture Definition Document, containing content updates:
Organization model for enterprise architecture	– Baseline Data Architecture
Tailored Architecture Framework	– Target Data Architecture
Data principles	– Data Architecture views corresponding to the selected viewpoints, addressing key stakeholder concerns
Statement of Architecture Work	Draft Architecture Requirements Specification, including content updates:
Architecture Vision	– Gap analysis results
Architecture Repository	– Data interoperability requirements
Draft Architecture Definition Document, containing:	– Relevant technical requirements that will apply to this evolution of the architecture development cycle
– Baseline Business Architecture (detailed)	– Constraints on the Technology Architecture
– Target Business Architecture (detailed)	– Updated business requirements
– Baseline Data Architecture (vision)	– Updated application requirements
– Target Data Architecture (vision)	Data Architecture components of an Architecture Roadmap
– Baseline Application Architecture (detailed or vision)	
– Target Application Architecture (detailed or vision)	
– Baseline Technology Architecture (vision)	
– Target Technology Architecture (vision)	
Draft Architecture Requirements Specification, including:	
– Gap analysis results	
– Relevant technical requirements Business Architecture components of an Architecture Roadmap	

2.3.4.2 Application Architecture

Objectives	Steps
Define the kinds of application systems necessary to process the data and support the business	Select reference models, viewpoints, and tools Develop Baseline Application Architecture Description Develop Target Application Architecture Description Perform gap analysis Define roadmap components Resolve impacts across the Architecture Landscape Conduct formal stakeholder review Finalize the Application Architecture Create Architecture Definition Document
Inputs	**Outputs**
Request for Architecture Work Capability Assessment Communications Plan Organization model for enterprise architecture Tailored Architecture Framework Application principles Statement of Architecture Work Architecture Vision Architecture Repository Draft Architecture Definition Document, containing: – Baseline Business Architecture (detailed) – Target Business Architecture (detailed) – Baseline Data Architecture (detailed or vision) – Target Data Architecture (detailed or vision) – Baseline Application Architecture (vision) – Target Application Architecture (vision) – Baseline Technology Architecture (vision) – Target Technology Architecture (vision) Draft Architecture Requirements Specification, including: – Gap analysis results – Relevant technical requirements Business and Data Architecture components of an Architecture Roadmap	Statement of Architecture Work, updated if necessary Validated application principles, or new application principles Draft Architecture Definition Document, containing content updates: – Baseline Application Architecture – Target Application Architecture – Application Architecture views corresponding to the selected viewpoints, addressing key stakeholder concerns Draft Architecture Requirements Specification, including content updates: – Gap analysis results – Application interoperability requirements – Relevant technical requirements that will apply to this evolution of the architecture development cycle – Constraints on the Technology Architecture – Updated business requirements – Updated data requirements Application Architecture components of an Architecture Roadmap

2.3.5 Phase D: Technology Architecture

Phase D is about documenting the fundamental organization of the
IT systems, embodied in the hardware, software, and communications
technology.

Objectives	Steps
To develop a Target Technology Architecture that will form the basis of the subsequent implementation and migration planning	Select reference models, viewpoints, and tools
	Develop Baseline Technology Architecture Description
	Develop Target Technology Architecture Description
	Perform gap analysis
	Define roadmap components
	Resolve impacts across the Architecture Landscape
	Conduct formal stakeholder review
	Finalize the Technology Architecture
	Create Architecture Definition Document
Inputs	**Outputs**
Request for Architecture Work	Statement of Architecture Work, updated if necessary
Capability Assessment	
Communications Plan	Validated technology principles or new technology principles (if generated here)
Organization model for enterprise architecture	
Tailored Architecture Framework	Draft Architecture Definition Document, containing content updates:
Technology principles	
Statement of Architecture Work	– Baseline Technology Architecture
Architecture Vision	– Target Technology Architecture
Architecture Repository	– Technology Architecture views corresponding to the selected viewpoints, addressing key stakeholder concerns
Draft Architecture Definition Document, containing:	
– Baseline Business Architecture (detailed)	
– Target Business Architecture (detailed)	Draft Architecture Requirements Specification, including content updates:
– Baseline Data Architecture (detailed)	– Gap analysis report
– Target Data Architecture (detailed)	– Requirements output from Phases B and C
– Baseline Application Architecture (detailed)	
– Target Application Architecture (detailed)	– Updated technology requirements
– Baseline Technology Architecture (vision)	Technology Architecture components of an Architecture Roadmap
– Target Technology Architecture (vision)	
Draft Architecture Requirements Specification, including:	
– Gap analysis results	
– Relevant technical requirements	
Business, Data, and Application Architecture components of an Architecture Roadmap	

2.3.6 Phase E: Opportunities and Solutions

Phase E is the first phase which is directly concerned with implementation. It describes the process of identifying delivery vehicles (projects, programs, or portfolios) that deliver the Target Architecture identified in previous phases.

Objectives	Steps
To review the target business objectives and capabilities, consolidate the gaps from Phases B to D, and then organize groups of building blocks to address these capabilities To confirm the enterprise's capability for undergoing change To derive a series of Transition Architectures that deliver continuous business value (e.g., capability increments) through the exploitation of opportunities to realize the building blocks To generate and gain consensus on an outline Implementation and Migration Strategy	Determine/confirm key corporate change attributes Determine business constraints for implementation Review and consolidate gap analysis results from Phases B to D Review IT requirements from a functional perspective Consolidate and reconcile interoperability requirements Refine and validate dependencies Confirm readiness and risk for business transformation Formulate high-level Implementation and Migration Strategy Identify and group major work packages Identify Transition Architectures Create portfolio and project charters and update the architectures

Inputs	Outputs
Product Information Request for Architecture Work Capability Assessment Communications Plan Planning Methodologies Organization model for enterprise architecture Tailored Architecture Framework Statement of Architecture Work Architecture Vision Architecture Repository Draft Architecture Definition Document Draft Architecture Requirements Specification Change Requests for existing programs and projects	Statement of Architecture Work, updated if necessary Architecture Vision, updated if necessary Draft Architecture Definition Document, including content updates for: – Identification of increments – Interoperability and co-existence requirements – Implementation and Migration Strategy – Inclusion of project list and project charters Draft Architecture Requirements Specification, updated if necessary Capability Assessment, including content updates for: – Enterprise Architecture Maturity Profile – Transformation Readiness Report Transition Architectures, including: – Consolidated Gaps, Solutions, and Dependencies Assessment – Risk Register – Impact analysis – project list – Dependency Analysis Report – Implementation Factor Assessment and Deduction Matrix Implementation and Migration Plan (outline)

2.3.7 Phase F: Migration Planning

Phase F addresses migration planning; that is, how to move from the Baseline to the Target Architectures by finalizing a detailed Implementation and Migration Plan.

Objectives	Steps
To ensure that the Implementation and Migration Plan is coordinated with the various management frameworks in use within the enterprise	Confirm management framework interactions for the Implementation and Migration Plan
To prioritize all work packages, projects, and building blocks by assigning business value to each and conducting a cost/business analysis	Assign a business value to each project
	Estimate resource requirements, project timings, and availability/delivery vehicle
To finalize the Architecture Vision and Architecture Definition Documents, in line with the agreed implementation approach	Prioritize the migration projects through the conduct of a cost/benefit assessment and risk validation
To confirm the Transition Architectures defined in Phase E with the relevant stakeholders	Confirm Transition Architecture increments/phases and update Architecture Definition Document
To create, evolve, and monitor the detailed Implementation and Migration Plan, providing necessary resources to enable the realization of the Transition Architectures, as defined in Phase E	Generate the Architecture Implementation Roadmap (time-lined) and Migration Plan
	Establish the architecture evolution cycle and document lessons learned

Inputs	Outputs
Request for Architecture Work	Implementation and Migration Plan (detailed)
Capability Assessment	Finalized Architecture Definition Document
Communications Plan	
Organization model for enterprise architecture	Finalized Architecture Requirements Specification
Governance Models and Frameworks	
Tailored Architecture Framework	Finalized Architecture Roadmap
Statement of Architecture Work	Transition Architecture
Architecture Vision	Re-Usable Architecture Building Blocks
Architecture Repository	
Draft Architecture Definition Document, including:	Requests for Architecture Work for the architecture aspects of implementation projects (if any)
– Strategic Migration Plan	
– Impact analysis – project list and charters	Architecture Contracts for implementation projects
Draft Architecture Requirements Specification	
Change Requests for existing programs and projects	Implementation Governance Model
Consolidated and validated Architecture Roadmap	Change Requests arising from lessons learned
Transition Architectures	
Implementation and Migration Plan (outline)	

2.3.8 Phase G: Implementation Governance

Phase G defines how the architecture constrains the implementation projects, monitors it while building it, and produces a signed Architecture Contract.

Objectives	Steps
Formulate recommendations for each implementation project	Confirm scope and priorities for deployment with development management
Govern and manage an Architecture Contract covering the overall implementation and deployment process	Identify deployment resources and skills
Perform appropriate governance functions while the system is being implemented and deployed	Guide development of solutions deployment
Ensure conformance with the defined architecture by implementation projects and other projects	Perform enterprise architecture compliance reviews
Ensure that the program of solutions is deployed successfully, as a planned program of work	Implement business and IT operations
Ensure conformance of the deployed solution with the Target Architecture	Perform post-implementation review and close the implementation
Mobilize supporting operations that will underpin the future working lifetime of the deployed solution	

Inputs	Outputs
Request for Architecture Work	Architecture Contract (signed)
Capability Assessment	Compliance Assessments
Organization model for enterprise architecture	Change Requests
Tailored Architecture Framework	Impact Analysis – Implementation Recommendations
Statement of Architecture Work	Architecture-compliant solutions deployed, including:
Architecture Vision	– The architecture-compliant implemented system
Architecture Repository	– Populated Architecture Repository
Architecture Definition Document	– Architecture compliance recommendations and dispensations
Architecture Requirements Specification	– Recommendations on service delivery requirements
Architecture Roadmap	– Recommendations on performance metrics
Transition Architecture	
Implementation Governance Model	– Service Level Agreements (SLAs)
Architecture Contract	– Architecture Vision, updated post-implementation
Request for Architecture Work identified in Phases E and F	– Architecture Definition Document, updated post-implementation
Implementation and Migration Plan	– Transition Architecture, updated post-implementation
	– Business and IT operating models for the implemented solution

2.3.9 Phase H: Architecture Change Management

Phase H ensures that changes to the architecture are managed in a controlled manner.

Objectives	Steps
Ensure that Baseline Architectures continue to be fit-for-purpose	Establish Value Realization process
Assess the performance of the architecture and make recommendations for change	Deploy Monitoring Tools
	Manage Risks
	Provide Analysis for Architecture Change Management
Assess changes to the framework and principles set up in previous phases	Develop Change Requirements to meet Performance Targets
Establish an architecture change management process for the new enterprise architecture baseline that is achieved with completion of Phase G	Manage Governance Process
	Activate the process to implement Change
Maximize the business value from the architecture and ongoing operations	
Operate the Governance Framework	

Inputs	Outputs
Request for Architecture Work identified in Phases E and F	Architecture updates
Organization model for enterprise architecture	Changes to architecture framework and principles
Tailored Architecture Framework	New Request for Architecture Work, to initiate another cycle of the ADM
Statement of Architecture Work	Statement of Architecture Work, updated if necessary
Architecture Vision	Architecture Contract, updated if necessary
Architecture Repository	Compliance Assessments, updated if necessary
Architecture Definition document	
Architecture Requirements Specification	
Architecture Roadmap	
Change Requests due to technology changes	
Change Requests due to business changes	
Change Requests from lessons learned	
Transition Architecture	
Implementation Governance Model	
Architecture Contract (signed)	
Compliance Assessments	
Implementation and Migration Plan	

2.3.10   Requirements Management

The process of managing architecture requirements applies to all phases of the ADM cycle. The Requirements Management process is a dynamic process, which addresses the identification of requirements for the enterprise, storing them, and then feeding them in and out of the relevant ADM phases. As shown in Figure 2, this process is central to driving the ADM process.

The ability to deal with changes in the requirements is crucial to the ADM process, since architecture by its very nature deals with uncertainty and change, bridging the divide between the aspirations of the stakeholders and what can be delivered as a practical solution.

Objectives	Steps
To provide a process to manage architecture requirements throughout the phases of the ADM cycle To identify requirements for the enterprise, store them, and feed them in and out of the relevant ADM phases, which dispose of, address, and prioritize requirements	Identify/document requirements Baseline requirements Monitor baseline requirements Identify changed requirements; remove, add, modify, and re-assess priorities Identify changed requirements and record priorities; identify and resolve conflicts; generate requirements impact statements Assess impact of changed requirements on current and previous ADM phases Implement requirements arising from Phase H Update the requirements repository Implement change in the current phase Assess and revise gap analysis for past phases

Inputs	Outputs
The inputs to the Requirements Management process are the requirements-related outputs from each ADM phase. The first high-level requirements are produced as part of the Architecture Vision. Each architecture domain then generates detailed requirements. Deliverables in later ADM phases contain mappings to new types of requirements (for example, conformance requirements).	Changed requirements Requirements Impact Assessment, which identifies the phases of the ADM that need to be revisited to address any changes. The final version must include the full implications of the requirements (e.g., costs, timescales, and business metrics).

2.4 Scoping the Architecture Activity

The ADM defines a recommended sequence for the various phases and steps involved in developing an organization-wide enterprise architecture, but the ADM cannot determine scope: this must be determined by the organization itself.

There are many reasons to constrain (or restrict) the scope of the architectural activity to be undertaken, most of which relate to limits in:

- The organizational authority of the team producing the architecture
- The objectives and stakeholder concerns to be addressed within the architecture
- The availability of people, finance, and other resources

The scope chosen for the architecture activity should ideally allow the work of all architects within the enterprise to be effectively governed and integrated. This requires a set of aligned "architecture partitions" that ensure architects are not working on duplicate or conflicting activities. It also requires the definition of re-use and compliance relationships between architecture partitions. The division of the enterprise and its architecture-related activity is addressed in TOGAF 9, Part III: ADM Guidelines and Techniques (see Chapter 4).

Table 4 shows the four dimensions in which the scope may be defined and limited.

Table 4: Dimensions for Limiting the Scope of the Architecture Activity

Dimension	Considerations
Enterprise Scope or Focus	What is the full extent of the enterprise, and how much of that extent should the architecting effort focus on? Many enterprises are very large, effectively comprising a federation of organizational units that could be considered enterprises in their own right. The modern enterprise increasingly extends beyond its traditional boundaries, to embrace a fuzzy combination of traditional business enterprise combined with suppliers, customers, and partners.
Architecture Domains	A complete enterprise architecture description should contain all four architecture domains (Business, Data, Application, Technology), but the realities of resource and time constraints often mean there is not enough time, funding, or resources to build a top-down, all-inclusive architecture description encompassing all four architecture domains, even if the enterprise scope is chosen to be less than the full extent of the overall enterprise.
Vertical Scope or Level of Detail	To what level of detail should the architecting effort go? How much architecture is "enough"? What is the appropriate demarcation between the architecture effort and other, related activities (system design, system engineering, system development)?
Time Period	What is the time period that needs to be articulated for the Architecture Vision, and does it make sense (in terms of practicality and resources) for the same period to be covered in the detailed architecture description? If not, how many intermediate Target Architectures are to be defined, and what are their time periods?

Chapter 3
Key Techniques and
Deliverables of the
ADM Cycle

This chapter will help you to understand the key techniques and deliverables of the ADM cycle. Table 5 gives a roadmap to this chapter by the ADM phase in which the techniques and deliverables are mainly used. For each point, key facts are presented.

Table 5: Roadmap to Chapter 3

ADM Phase	Reference(s)
Preliminary	Section 3.1, Tailored Architecture Framework
	Section 3.2, Organizational Model for Enterprise Architecture
	Section 3.3, Architecture Principles
	Section 3.4, Business Principles, Business Goals, and Business Drivers
	Section 3.5, Architecture Repository
	Section 3.6, Architecture Tools
	Section 3.7, Request for Architecture Work
A. Architecture Vision	Section 3.4, Business Principles, Business Goals, and Business Drivers
	Section 3.8, Statement of Architecture Work
	Section 3.9, Architecture Vision
	Section 3.10, Stakeholder Management
	Section 3.11, Communications Plan
	Section 3.12, Business Transformation Readiness Assessment
	Section 3.13, Capability Assessment
	Section 3.14, Risk Management
	Section 3.18, Business Scenarios
	Section 3.20, Architecture Viewpoints
	Section 3.21, Architecture Views

ADM Phase	Reference(s)
B. Business Architecture	Section 3.15, Architecture Definition Document
	Section 3.16, Architecture Requirements Specification
	Section 3.17, Architecture Roadmap
	Section 3.18, Business Scenarios
	Section 3.19, Gap Analysis
	Section 3.20, Architecture Viewpoints
	Section 3.21, Architecture Views
	Section 3.22, Architecture Building Blocks
	Section 3.23, Solution Building Blocks
C. Information Systems Architectures	Section 3.15, Architecture Definition Document
	Section 3.16, Architecture Requirements Specification
	Section 3.17, Architecture Roadmap
	Section 3.19, Gap Analysis
	Section 3.20, Architecture Viewpoints
	Section 3.21, Architecture Views
	Section 3.22, Architecture Building Blocks
	Section 3.23, Solution Building Blocks
D. Technology Architecture	Section 3.15, Architecture Definition Document
	Section 3.16, Architecture Requirements Specification
	Section 3.17, Architecture Roadmap
	Section 3.19, Gap Analysis
	Section 3.20, Architecture Viewpoints
	Section 3.21, Architecture Views
	Section 3.22, Architecture Building Blocks
	Section 3.23, Solution Building Blocks
E. Opportunities and Solutions	Section 3.13, Capability Assessment
	Section 3.17, Architecture Roadmap
	Section 3.19, Gap Analysis
	Section 3.22, Architecture Building Blocks
	Section 3.23, Solution Building Blocks
	Section 3.24, Capability-Based Planning
	Section 3.25, Migration Planning Techniques
	Section 3.26, Implementation and Migration Plan
	Section 3.27, Transition Architecture
	Section 3.28, Implementation Governance Model

ADM Phase	Reference(s)
F. Migration Planning	Section 3.17, Architecture Roadmap
	Section 3.24, Capability-Based Planning
	Section 3.25, Migration Planning Techniques
	Section 3.26, Implementation and Migration Plan
	Section 3.27, Transition Architecture
	Section 3.28, Implementation Governance Model
G. Implementation Governance	Section 3.28, Implementation Governance Model
	Section 3.29, Architecture Contracts
	Section 3.30, Change Request
	Section 3.31, Compliance Assessment
H. Architecture Change Management	Section 3.28, Implementation Governance Model
	Section 3.29, Architecture Contracts
	Section 3.30, Change Request
	Section 3.31, Compliance Assessment
	Section 3.32, Requirements Impact Assessment

3.1 Tailored Architecture Framework

Preliminary

Selecting and tailoring a framework is the practical starting point for an architecture project. Building on TOGAF has a number of advantages over creating a framework from scratch:

- It avoids the initial panic when the scale of the task becomes apparent.
- Use of TOGAF is systematic – "codified common sense".
- TOGAF captures what others have found to work in real life.
- TOGAF has a baseline set of resources to re-use.
- TOGAF defines two reference architectures in the Enterprise Continuum.

However, before TOGAF can be effectively used within an architecture project, tailoring at a number of levels is necessary and should occur in the Preliminary phase.

Firstly, it is necessary to tailor the TOGAF model for integration into the enterprise. This tailoring will include integration with project and process management frameworks, customization of terminology, development of presentational styles, selection, configuration, and deployment of architecture tools, etc. The formality and detail of any frameworks adopted should also align with other contextual factors for the enterprise, such as culture, stakeholders, commercial models for enterprise architecture, and the existing level of architecture capability.

Once the framework has been tailored to the enterprise, further tailoring is necessary in order to tailor the framework for the specific architecture project. Tailoring at this level will select appropriate deliverables and artifacts to meet project and stakeholder needs.

The following contents are typical within a Tailored Architecture Framework:

- Tailored architecture method
- Tailored architecture content (deliverables and artifacts)
- Configured and deployed tools
- Interfaces with governance models and other frameworks:
    - Enterprise Architecture Management Framework
    - Capability Management Framework
    - Portfolio Management Framework
    - Project Management Framework
    - Operations Management Framework

3.2 Organizational Model for Enterprise Architecture

An important deliverable produced in the Preliminary phase is the Organizational Model for Enterprise Architecture.

In order for an architecture framework to be used successfully, it must be supported by the correct organization, roles, and responsibilities within the enterprise. Of particular importance is the definition of boundaries between different enterprise architecture practitioners and the governance relationships that span across these boundaries.

Typical contents of an Organizational Model for Enterprise Architecture are:
- Scope of organizations impacted
- Maturity assessment, gaps, and resolution approach
- Roles and responsibilities for architecture team(s)
- Constraints on architecture work
- Budget requirements
- Governance and support strategy

3.3 Architecture Principles

This set of documentation is an initial output of the Preliminary phase. It is the set of general rules and guidelines for the architecture being developed. See TOGAF 9, Part III, Architecture Principles for guidelines and a detailed set of generic architecture principles. The suggested contents of this document are business principles, data principles, application principles, and technology principles.

3.3.1 Developing Architecture Principles

The Lead Architect, in conjunction with the enterprise CIO, Architecture Board, and other key business stakeholders, typically develops architecture principles.

The following typically influences the development of architecture principles:
- **Enterprise mission and plans**: The mission, plans, and organizational infrastructure of the enterprise.
- **Enterprise strategic initiatives**: The characteristics of the enterprise – its strengths, weaknesses, opportunities, and threats – and its current enterprise-wide initiatives (such as process improvement and quality management).

- **External constraints**: Market factors (time-to-market imperatives, customer expectations, etc.); existing and potential legislation.
- **Current systems and technology**: The set of information resources deployed within the enterprise, including systems documentation, equipment inventories, network configuration diagrams, policies, and procedures.
- **Computer industry trends**: Predictions about the usage, availability, and cost of computer and communication technologies, taken from credible sources along with associated best practices presently in use.

3.3.2 Defining Architecture Principles

Depending on the organization, principles may be established at any or all of three levels:

- **Enterprise principles** provide a basis for decision-making and dictate how the organization fulfills its mission. Such principles are commonly found in governmental and not-for-profit organizations, but are also found in commercial organizations, as a means of harmonizing decision-making. They are a key element in a successful architecture governance strategy.
- **IT principles** provide guidance on the use and deployment of all IT resources and assets across the enterprise. They are developed to make the information environment as productive and cost-effective as possible.
- **Architecture principles** are a subset of IT principles that relate to architecture work. They reflect consensus across the enterprise, and embody the spirit of the enterprise architecture. Architecture principles can be further divided into:
  - Principles that govern the architecture process, affecting the development, maintenance, and use of the enterprise architecture
  - Principles that govern the implementation of the architecture

TOGAF defines a standard way of describing principles. In addition to a definition statement, each principle should have associated rationale and implications statements, both to promote understanding and acceptance of the principles themselves, and to support the use of the principles in explaining and justifying why specific decisions are made.

Table 6: TOGAF Template for Defining Principles

Name	Should both represent the essence of the rule as well as be easy to remember. Specific technology platforms should not be mentioned in the name or statement of a principle. Avoid ambiguous words in the name and in the statement such as: "support", "open", "consider", and for lack of good measure the word "avoid", itself, be careful with "manage(ment)", and look for unnecessary adjectives and adverbs (fluff).
Statement	Should succinctly and unambiguously communicate the fundamental rule. For the most part, the principles statements for managing information are similar among organizations. It is vital that the principles statement be unambiguous.
Rationale	Should highlight the business benefits of adhering to the principle, using business terminology. Point to the similarity of information and technology principles to the principles governing business operations. Also describe the relationship to other principles, and the intentions regarding a balanced interpretation. Describe situations where one principle would be given precedence or carry more weight than another for making a decision.
Implications	Should highlight the requirements, both for the business and IT, for carrying out the principle – in terms of resources, costs, and activities/tasks. It will often be apparent that current systems, standards, or practices would be incongruent with the principle upon adoption. The impact on the business and consequences of adopting a principle should be clearly stated. The reader should readily discern the answer to: "How does this affect me?" It is important not to oversimplify, trivialize, or judge the merit of the impact. Some of the implications will be identified as potential impacts only, and may be speculative rather than fully analyzed.

3.3.3 Qualities of Principles

There are five criteria that distinguish a good set of principles, as shown in Table 7.

Table 7: Recommended Criteria for Quality Principles

Criteria	Description
Understandability	The underlying tenets of a principle can be quickly grasped and understood by individuals throughout the organization. The intention of the principle is clear and unambiguous, so that violations, whether intentional or not, are minimized.
Robustness	Principles should enable good quality decisions about architectures and plans to be made, and enforceable policies and standards to be created. Each principle should be sufficiently definitive and precise to support consistent decision-making in complex, potentially controversial situations.
Completeness	Every potentially important principle governing the management of information and technology for the organization is defined. The principles cover every situation perceived.
Consistency	Strict adherence to one principle may require a loose interpretation of another principle. The set of principles must be expressed in a way that allows a balance of interpretations. Principles should not be contradictory to the point where adhering to one principle would violate the spirit of another. Every word in a principle statement should be carefully chosen to allow consistent yet flexible interpretation.
Stability	Principles should be enduring, yet able to accommodate changes. An amendment process should be established for adding, removing, or altering principles after they are ratified initially.

3.3.4 Applying Architecture Principles

Architecture principles are used to capture the fundamental truths about how the enterprise will use and deploy IT resources and assets. The principles are used in a number of different ways:

1. To provide a framework within which the enterprise can start to make conscious decisions about IT

2. As a guide to establishing relevant evaluation criteria, thus exerting strong influence on the selection of products or product architectures in the later stages of managing compliance to the IT architecture

3. As drivers for defining the functional requirements of the architecture

4. As an input to assessing both existing IS/IT systems and the future strategic portfolio, for compliance with the defined architectures; these assessments will provide valuable insights into the transition activities needed to implement an architecture, in support of business goals and priorities

5. The Rationale statements highlight the value of the architecture to the enterprise, and therefore provide a basis for justifying architecture activities

6. The Implications statements provide an outline of the key tasks, resources, and potential costs to the enterprise of following the principle; they also provide valuable inputs to future transition initiatives and planning activities

7. To support the architecture governance activities in terms of:
   – Providing a "back-stop" for the standard Architecture Compliance assessments where some interpretation is allowed or required
   – Supporting a decision to initiate a dispensation request where the implications of a particular architecture amendment cannot be resolved within local operating procedure

Principles are inter-related, and need to be applied as a set. Principles will sometimes compete; for example, the principles of "accessibility" and "security". Each principle must be considered in the context of "all other things being equal". At times a decision will be required as to which principle will take precedence on a particular issue. The rationale for such decisions should always be documented. The fact that a principle seems self-evident does not mean that the principle is actually observed in an organization, even when there are verbal acknowledgements of the principle. Although specific penalties are not prescribed in a declaration of principles, violations of principles generally cause operational problems and inhibit the ability of the organization to fulfill its mission.

3.4 Business Principles, Business Goals, and Business Drivers

A statement of the business principles, goals, and drivers has usually been defined elsewhere in the enterprise prior to the architecture activity. They are restated as an output of the Preliminary phase and reviewed again as a part of Phase A: Architecture Vision. The activity in Phase A is to ensure that the current definitions are correct and clear. TOGAF 9, Part III: ADM Guidelines and Techniques contains an example set of eight business principles that are a useful starting point.

There is no defined content for this deliverable as its content and structure is likely to vary considerably from one organization to the next.

3.5 Architecture Repository

The Architecture Repository acts as a holding area for all architecture-related projects within the enterprise. The repository allows projects to manage their deliverables, locate re-usable assets, and publish outputs to stakeholders and other interested parties. See Section 6.2 for a description of the content of an Architecture Repository. The following contents are typical within an Architecture Repository:

- Architecture Framework
- Standards Information Base
- Architecture Landscape
- Reference Architectures
- Governance Log

3.6 Architecture Tools

As part of the Preliminary phase, the architect should select and implement tools to support the architecture activity. TOGAF does not require or recommend any specific tool. TOGAF provides a set of proposed evaluation criteria for selecting architecture tools to develop the various architecture models and views that are required. These are documented in TOGAF 9, Part V, Chapter 42.

3.7 Request for Architecture Work

This is a document that is sent from the sponsoring organization to the architecture organization to trigger the start of an architecture development cycle. It is produced with the assistance of the architecture organization as an output of the Preliminary phase. Requests for Architecture Work will also be created as a result of approved architecture Change Requests, or terms of reference for architecture work originating from migration planning.

In general, all the information in this document should be at a high level. The suggested contents of this document are as follows:

- Organization sponsors
- Organization's mission statement
- Business goals (and changes)
- Strategic plans of the business
- Time limits
- Changes in the business environment
- Organizational constraints
- Budget information, financial constraints
- External constraints, business constraints
- Current business system description
- Current architecture/IT system description
- Description of developing organization
- Description of resources available to developing organization

3.8 Statement of Architecture Work

The Statement of Architecture Work is created as a deliverable of Phase A, and is effectively a contract between the architecting organization and the sponsor of the architecture project. This document is a response to the Request for Architecture Work input document (see Section 3.6). It should describe an overall plan to address the request for work and propose how solutions to the problems that have been identified will be addressed through the architecture process. The suggested contents of this document are as follows:

- Statement of work title
- Project request and background
- Project description and scope
- Overview or outline of Architecture Vision
- Managerial approach
- Change of scope procedures
- Responsibilities and deliverables
- Acceptance criteria and procedures
- Project plan and schedule
- Support of the Enterprise Continuum (re-use)
- Signature approvals

3.9 Architecture Vision

The Architecture Vision is created in Phase A and provides a high-level, aspirational view of the end architecture product. The purpose of the vision is to agree at the outset what the desired outcome should be for the architecture, so that architects can then focus on the critical areas to validate feasibility. Providing an Architecture Vision also supports stakeholder communication by providing an executive summary version of the full Architecture Definition.

Business scenarios are an appropriate and important technique that can be used as part of the process in developing an Architecture Vision document.

The suggested contents are as follows:
- Problem description:
  - Stakeholders and their concerns
  - List of issues/scenarios to be addressed
- Detailed objectives
- Environment and process models:
  - Process description
  - Process steps mapped to environment
  - Process steps mapped to people
  - Information flow
- Actors and their roles and responsibilities:
  - Human actors and roles
  - Computer actors and roles
  - Requirements
- Resulting architecture model:
  - Constraints
  - IT principles
  - Architecture supporting the process
  - Requirements mapped to architecture

3.10 Stakeholder Management

Stakeholder management is an important discipline that successful architects can use to win support from others. It helps them ensure that their projects succeed where others fail. The technique should be used during Phase A to identify the key players in the engagement, and also be updated throughout each phase. The output of this process forms the start of the Communications Plan (see Section 3.11).

The benefits of successful stakeholder management are that:

- The most powerful stakeholders can be identified early and their input can then be used to shape the architecture; this ensures their support and improves the quality of the models produced.
- Support from the more powerful stakeholders will help the engagement win more resource[s]; thus making the architecture engagement more likely to succeed.
- By communicating with stakeholders early and frequently, the architecture team can ensure that they fully understand the architecture process, and the benefits of enterprise architecture; this means they can support the architecture team more actively when necessary.
- The architecture engagement team can more effectively anticipate likely reactions to the architecture models and reports, and can build into the plan the actions that will be needed to capitalize on positive reaction whilst avoiding or addressing any negative reactions.

3.10.1   Steps in the Stakeholder Management Process

Step 1: Identify Stakeholders

The first task is to determine who the main enterprise architecture stakeholders are.

It is possible to distinguish five broad categories of stakeholder, as shown in Figure 3.

Step 2: Classify Stakeholder Positions

Develop a good understanding of the most important stakeholders and record this analysis (as shown in the example in Table 8) for reference and refresh during the project.

Step 3: Determine Stakeholder Management Approach

This step enables the team to easily see which stakeholders are expected to be blockers or critics, and which stakeholders are likely to be advocates and supporters of the initiative.

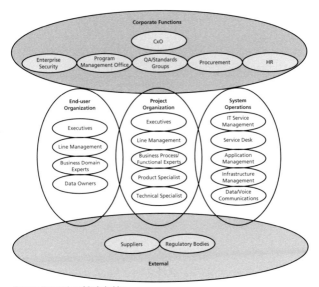

Figure 3: Categories of Stakeholder

Table 8: Example Stakeholder Analysis

Stake-holder Group	Stake-holder	Ability to Disrupt the Change	Current Under-standing	Required Under-standing	Current Commit-ment	Required Commit-ment	Required Support
CIO	John Smith	H	M	H	L	M	H
CFO	Jeff Brown	M	M	M	L	M	M

Work out stakeholder power, influence, and interest, so as to focus the enterprise architecture engagement on the key individuals. These can be mapped onto a power/interest matrix, which also indicates the strategy you need to adopt for engaging with them.

Figure 4 shows an example power grid matrix.

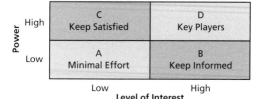

Figure 4: Power Grid

Step 4: Tailor Engagement Deliverables
Identify viewpoints, matrices, and views that the architecture engagement needs to produce and validate with each stakeholder group to deliver an effective architecture model.

It is important to pay particular attention to stakeholder interests by defining specific viewpoints, matrices, and views of the enterprise architecture model. This enables the architecture to be communicated to, and understood by, all the stakeholders, and enables them to verify that the enterprise architecture initiative will address their concerns.

3.11 Communications Plan
Enterprise architectures contain large volumes of complex and inter-dependent information. Effective communication of targeted information to the right stakeholders at the right time is a critical success factor for enterprise architecture. Development of a Communications Plan for architecture in Phase A allows for this communication to be carried out within a planned and managed process.

Typical contents of a Communications Plan are:
• Identification of stakeholders and grouping by communication requirements

- Identification of communication needs, key messages in relation to the Architecture Vision, communication risks, and Critical Success Factors (CSFs)
- Identification of mechanisms that will be used to communicate with stakeholders and allow access to architecture information, such as meetings, newsletters, repositories, etc.
- Identification of a communications timetable, showing which communications will occur with which stakeholder groups at what time and in what location

A. Architecture Vision

3.12 Business Transformation Readiness Assessment

The technique known as Business Transformation Readiness Assessment is carried out in Phase A and is used for evaluating and quantifying an organization's readiness to undergo change. Understanding the readiness of the organization to accept change, identifying the issues, and then dealing with them is a key part of successful architecture transformation. This assessment is recommended to be a joint effort between corporate staff, lines of business, and IT planners.

The recommended activities are:
- Determine the readiness factors that will impact the organization
- Present the readiness factors using maturity models
- Assess the risks for each readiness factor and identify improvement actions to mitigate the risk

Document the findings into the Capability Assessment (see Section 3.13), and later incorporate the actions into the Implementation and Migration Plan.

3.13 Capability Assessment

Before embarking upon a detailed Architecture Definition, it is valuable to understand the baseline and target capability level of the enterprise. This Capability Assessment is first carried out in Phase A, and updated in Phase E. It can be examined on several levels:

- What is the capability level of the enterprise as a whole? Where does the enterprise wish to increase or optimize capability? What are the architectural focus areas that will support the desired development of the enterprise?

- What is the capability or maturity level of the IT function within the enterprise? What are the likely implications of conducting the architecture project in terms or design governance, operational governance, skills, and organization structure? What is an appropriate style, level of formality, and amount of detail for the architecture project to fit with the culture and capability of the IT organization?

- What is the capability and maturity of the architecture function within the enterprise? What architectural assets are currently in existence? Are they maintained and accurate? What standards and reference models need to be considered? Are there likely to be opportunities to create re-usable assets during the architecture project?

- Where capability gaps exist, to what extent is the business ready to transform in order to reach the target capability? What are the risks to transformation, cultural barriers, and other considerations to be addressed beyond the basic capability gap?

The following contents are typical within a Capability Assessment deliverable:

- Business Capability Assessment, including:
  - Capabilities of the business
  - Baseline state assessment of the performance level of each capability
  - Future state aspiration for the performance level of each capability
  - Baseline state assessment of how each capability is realized

- Future state aspiration for how each capability should be realized
- IT Capability Assessment, including:
  - Baseline and target maturity level of change process
  - Baseline and target maturity level of operational processes
  - Baseline capability and capacity assessment
  - Assessment of likely impacts to the IT organization resulting from execution of the architecture project
- Architecture Maturity Assessment, including:
  - Architecture governance processes, organization, roles, and responsibilities
  - Architecture skills assessment
  - Breadth, depth, and quality of landscape definition within the Architecture Repository
  - Breadth, depth, and quality of standards definition within the Architecture Repository
  - Breadth, depth, and quality of reference model definition within the Architecture Repository
  - Assessment of re-use potential
- Business Transformation Readiness Assessment, including:
  - Readiness factors
  - Vision for each readiness factor
  - Current and target readiness ratings
  - Readiness risks

3.14 Risk Management

Identification of business transformation risks and mitigation activities is first determined in Phase A. Risk management, documented in TOGAF 9, Part III, Chapter 31, is a technique used to mitigate risk when implementing an architecture project. It includes a process for managing risk consisting of the following activities:

- Risk classification
- Risk identification
- Initial risk assessment

- Risk mitigation and residual risk assessment
- Risk monitoring

It is recommended that risk mitigation activities be included within the Statement of Architecture Work.

3.15 Architecture Definition Document

The Architecture Definition Document is the deliverable container for the core architectural artifacts created during a project. The Architecture Definition Document spans all architecture domains (Business, Data, Application, and Technology) and also examines all relevant states of the architecture (baseline, interim state(s), and target).

It is first created in Phase B, populated initially with Business Architecture-related material, and subsequently updated with Information Systems Architecture material in Phase C, and then with Technology Architecture material in Phase D.

The Architecture Definition Document is a companion to the Architecture Requirements Specification, with a complementary objective:
- The Architecture Definition Document provides a qualitative view of the solution and aims to communicate the intent of the architects.
- The Architecture Requirements Specification provides a quantitative view of the solution, stating measurable criteria that must be met during the implementation of the architecture.

The following contents are typically found within an Architecture Definition Document:
- Scope
- Goals, objectives, and constraints

- Architecture principles
- Baseline Architecture
- Architecture models (for each state to be modeled):
  - Business Architecture models
  - Data Architecture models
  - Application Architecture models
  - Technology Architecture models
- Rationale and justification for architectural approach
- Mapping to Architecture Repository:
  - Mapping to Architecture Landscape
  - Mapping to reference models
  - Mapping to standards
  - Re-use assessment
- Gap analysis
- Impact assessment

The following sections look at each of the architectures in more detail.

3.15.1 Business Architecture

The Business Architecture is developed in Phase B. The topics that should be addressed in the Architecture Definition Document related to Business Architecture are as follows:

- Baseline Business Architecture, if appropriate – this is a description of the existing Business Architecture
- Target Business Architecture, including:
  - Organization structure – identifying business locations and relating them to organizational units
  - Business goals and objectives – for the enterprise and each organizational unit
  - Business functions – a detailed, recursive step involving successive decomposition of major functional areas into sub-functions

- Business services – the services that the enterprise and each enterprise unit provides to its customers, both internally and externally
- Business processes, including measures and deliverables
- Business roles, including development and modification of skills requirements
- Business data model
- Correlation of organization and functions – relate business functions to organizational units in the form of a matrix report
- Views corresponding to the selected viewpoints addressing key stakeholder concerns

3.15.2   Information Systems Architectures

The Information Systems Architectures are developed in Phase C. The topics that should be addressed in the Architecture Definition Document related to the Information Systems Architectures are as follows:

- Baseline Data Architecture, if appropriate
- Target Data Architecture, including:
  - Business data model
  - Logical data model
  - Data management process models
  - Data Entity/Business Function matrix
- Data Architecture views corresponding to the selected viewpoints addressing key stakeholder concerns
- Baseline Application Architecture, if appropriate
- Target Application Architecture, including:
  - Process systems model
  - Place systems model
  - Time systems model
  - People systems model
- Application Architecture views corresponding to the selected viewpoints addressing key stakeholder concerns

3.15.3 Technology Architecture

The Technology Architecture is developed as part of Phase D. The topics that should be addressed in the Architecture Definition Document related to Technology Architecture are as follows:

- Baseline Technology Architecture, if appropriate
- Target Technology Architecture, including:
  - Technology components and their relationships to information systems
  - Technology platforms and their decomposition, showing the combinations of technology required to realize a particular technology "stack"
  - Environments and locations – a grouping of the required technology into computing environments (e.g., development, production)
  - Expected processing load and distribution of load across technology components
  - Physical (network) communications
  - Hardware and network specifications
- Views corresponding to the selected viewpoints addressing key stakeholder concerns

3.16 Architecture Requirements Specification

The Architecture Requirements Specification provides a set of quantitative statements that outline what an implementation project must do in order to comply with the architecture. An Architecture Requirements Specification will typically form a major component of an implementation contract or contract for more detailed architecture definition.

As mentioned above, the Architecture Requirements Specification is a companion to the Architecture Definition Document, with a complementary objective to provide the quantitative view.

The following contents are typical within an Architecture Requirements Specification:

- Success measures
- Architecture requirements
- Business service contracts
- Application service contracts
- Implementation guidelines
- Implementation specifications
- Implementation standards
- Interoperability requirements (see Section 3.16.4)
- Constraints
- Assumptions

3.16.1   Business Architecture Requirements

Business Architecture requirements populating the Architecture Requirements Specification in Phase B include:

- Gap analysis results
- Technical requirements

   An initial set of technical requirements should be generated as the output of Phase B (Business Architecture). These are the drivers for the Technology Architecture work that follows, and should identify, categorize, and prioritize the implications for work in the remaining architecture domains; for example, by a dependency/priority matrix (e.g., guiding trade-off between speed of transaction processing and security); list the specific models that are expected to be produced (e.g., expressed as primitives of the Zachman Framework).

- Updated business requirements

   The business scenarios technique is used to discover and document business requirements.

3.16.2   Information Systems Architectures Requirements

Information Systems Architectures requirements populating the
Architecture Requirements Specification in Phase C include:

- Gap analysis results
- Data interoperability requirements
- Application interoperability requirements
- Areas where the Business Architecture may need to change in order to
  comply with changes in the Data and/or Application Architecture
- Constraints on the Technology Architecture about to be designed
- Updated business requirements, if appropriate
- Updated application requirements, if appropriate
- Updated data requirements, if appropriate

3.16.3   Technology Architecture Requirements

Technology Architecture requirements populating the Architecture
Requirements Specification in Phase D include:

- Gap analysis results
- Updated technology requirements

3.16.4   Interoperability Requirements

The determination of interoperability is present throughout the ADM
cycle. A set of guidelines is provided in TOGAF 9, Part III, Chapter 29, for
defining and establishing interoperability requirements.

3.17 Architecture Roadmap

The Architecture Roadmap lists individual increments
of change and lays them out on a timeline to show
progression from the Baseline Architecture to the Target
Architecture. The Architecture Roadmap forms a key
component of Transition Architectures and is incrementally developed
throughout Phases B, C, D, E, and F within the ADM.

The following contents are typically found within an Architecture
Roadmap:

- Project list:
  - Name, description, and objectives of each project
  - Prioritized list of projects to implement the proposed architecture
- Time-oriented Migration Plan:
  - Benefits of migration determined (including mapping to business
    requirements)
  - Estimated costs of migration options
- Implementation recommendations:
  - Criteria/measures of effectiveness of projects
  - Risks and issues
  - Solution Building Blocks (SBBs) – description and model

3.18 Business Scenarios

The ADM has its own method (a "method-within-a-method") for identifying and articulating the
business requirements implied in new business
functionality to address key business drivers, and the implied architecture
requirements. This process is known as "business scenarios".

A business scenario is a description of a business problem, which enables
requirements to be viewed in relation to one another in the context of
the overall problem. Without such a description to serve as context, the
business value of solving the problem is unclear, the relevance of potential
solutions is unclear, and there is a danger of the solution being based on an
inadequate set of requirements.

A key factor in the success of any other major project is the extent to which
it is linked to business requirements, and demonstrably supports and
enables the enterprise to achieve its business objectives. Business scenarios
are an important technique to help identify and understand business needs.

The technique may be used iteratively, at different levels of detail in the hierarchical decomposition of the Business Architecture. The generic business scenario process is as follows:

- Identify, document, and rank the problem that is driving the project
- Document, as high-level architecture models, the business and technical environments where the problem situation is occurring
- Identify and document desired objectives; the results of handling the problems successfully
- Identify human actors and their place in the business model, the human participants, and their roles
- Identify computer actors and their place in the technology model, the computing elements, and their roles
- Identify and document roles, responsibilities, and measures of success per actor, the required scripts per actor, and the desired results of handling the situation properly
- Check for fitness-for-purpose of inspiring subsequent architecture work, and refine only if necessary

3.19 Gap Analysis

The technique known as gap analysis is widely used in the ADM to validate an architecture that is being developed. It is usually the final step within a phase. The basic premise is to highlight a shortfall between the Baseline Architecture and the Target Architecture; that is, items that have been deliberately omitted, accidentally left out, or not yet defined.

The steps are as follows:

- Draw up a matrix with all the Architecture Building Blocks (ABBs) of the Baseline Architecture on the vertical axis, and all the ABBs of the Target Architecture on the horizontal axis.
- Add to the Baseline Architecture axis a final row labeled "New ABBs", and to the Target Architecture axis a final column labeled "Eliminated ABBs".

- Where an ABB is available in both the Baseline and Target Architectures, record this with "Included" at the intersecting cell.
- Where an ABB from the Baseline Architecture is missing in the Target Architecture, each must be reviewed. If it was correctly eliminated, mark it as such in the appropriate "Eliminated" cell. If it was not, you have uncovered an accidental omission in your Target Architecture that must be addressed by reinstating the ABB in the next iteration of the architecture design – mark it as such in the appropriate "Eliminated" cell.
- Where an ABB from the Target Architecture cannot be found in the Baseline Architecture, mark it at the intersection with the "New" row as a gap that needs to filled, either by developing or procuring the building block.

When the exercise is complete, anything under "Eliminated Services" or "New Services" is a gap, which should either be explained as correctly eliminated, or marked as to be addressed by reinstating or developing/procuring the function.

Table 9 shows examples of gaps between the Baseline Architecture and the Target Architecture; in this case the missing elements are "broadcast services" and "shared screen services".

Table 9: Gap Analysis Example

Target Architecture → Baseline Architecture ↓	Video Conferencing Services	Enhanced Telephony Services	Mailing List Services	Eliminated Services ↓
Broadcast Services				Intentionally Eliminated

Video Conferencing Services	Included			
Enhanced Telephony Services		Potential Match		
Shared Screen Services				Unintentionally excluded – a gap in Target Architecture
New →		Gap: Enhanced services to be developed or produced	Gap: Enhanced services to be developed or produced	

The gap analysis technique should be used in Phases B, C, D, and E of the ADM.

3.20 Architecture Viewpoints

The architect uses views and viewpoints in the ADM cycle during Phases A through D for developing architectures for each domain (Business, Data, Application, Technology). A "view" is what you see. A "viewpoint" is where you are looking from; the vantage point or perspective that determines what you see (a viewpoint can also be thought of as a schema). Viewpoints are generic, and can be stored in libraries for re-use. A view is always specific to the architecture for which it is created. Every view has an associated viewpoint that describes it, at least implicitly.

ISO/IEC 42010:2007 encourages architects to define viewpoints explicitly. Making this distinction between the content and schema of a view may seem at first to be an unnecessary overhead, but it provides a mechanism for re-using viewpoints across different architectures.

To illustrate the concepts of views and viewpoints, consider Example 1. This is a very simple airport system with two different stakeholders: the pilot and the air traffic controller.

Example 1: Views and Viewpoints for a Simple Airport System

> ### Views and Viewpoints for a Simple Airport System
>
> The pilot has one view of the system, and the air traffic controller has another. Neither view represents the whole system, because the perspective of each stakeholder constrains (and reduces) how each sees the overall system.
>
> The view of the pilot comprises some elements not viewed by the controller, such as passengers and fuel, while the view of the controller comprises some elements not viewed by the pilot, such as other planes. There are also elements shared between the views, such as the communication model between the pilot and the controller, and the vital information about the plane itself.
>
> A viewpoint is a model (or description) of the information contained in a view. In this example, one viewpoint is the description of how the pilot sees the system, and the other viewpoint is how the controller sees the system. Pilots describe the system from their perspective, using

a model of their position and vector toward or away from the runway. All pilots use this model, and the model has a specific language that is used to capture information and populate the model. Controllers describe the system differently, using a model of the airspace and the locations and vectors of aircraft within the airspace. Again, all controllers use a common language derived from the common model in order to capture and communicate information pertinent to their viewpoint.

Fortunately, when controllers talk with pilots, they use a common communication language. (In other words, the models representing their individual viewpoints partially intersect.) Part of this common language is about location and vectors of aircraft, and is essential to safety. So in essence each viewpoint is an abstract model of how all the stakeholders of a particular type – all pilots, or all controllers – view the airport system. The interface to the human user of a tool is typically close to the model and language associated with the viewpoint. The unique tools of the pilot are fuel, altitude, speed, and location indicators. The main tool of the controller is radar. The common tool is a radio.

To summarize from Example 1, we can see that a view can subset the system through the perspective of the stakeholder, such as the pilot *versus* the controller. This subset can be described by an abstract model called a viewpoint, such as an air flight *versus* an air space model. This description of the view is documented in a partially specialized language, such as "pilot-speak" *versus* "controller-speak". Tools are used to assist the stakeholders, and they interface with each other in terms of the language derived from the viewpoint. When stakeholders use common tools, such as the radio contact between pilot and controller, a common language is essential.

3.21 Architecture Views

Architecture views are representations of the overall architecture that are meaningful to one or more stakeholders in the system. The architect chooses and develops a set of views in the ADM cycle during Phases A through D that enable the architecture to be communicated to, and understood by, all the stakeholders, and enable them to verify that the system will address their concerns. The concepts in Section 5.3 are central to the use of architecture views within TOGAF.

3.21.1   Developing Views in the ADM

The choice of which particular architecture views to develop is one of the key decisions that the architect has to make.

The architect has a responsibility for ensuring the completeness (fitness-for-purpose) of the architecture, in terms of adequately addressing all the pertinent concerns of its stakeholders; and the integrity of the architecture, in terms of connecting all the various views to each other, satisfactorily reconciling the conflicting concerns of different stakeholders, and showing the trade-offs made in so doing (as between security and performance, for example).

3.22 Architecture Building Blocks

Architecture Building Blocks (ABBs) are architecture documentation and models from the enterprise's Architecture Repository classified according to the Architecture Continuum (see Chapter 6). They are defined or selected during application of the ADM (mainly in Phases A, B, C, and D). The characteristics of ABBs are as follows:

- They capture architecture requirements; e.g., business, data, application, and technology requirements.
- They direct and guide the development of Solution Building Blocks (SBBs).

The content of ABB specifications includes the following as a minimum:

- Fundamental functionality and attributes: semantics, unambiguous, including security capability and manageability
- Interfaces: chosen set, supplied (APIs, data formats, protocols, hardware interfaces, standards)
- Interoperability and relationship with other building blocks
- Dependent building blocks with required functionality and named user interfaces
- Map to business/organizational entities and policies

Each ABB should include a statement of any architecture documentation and models from the enterprise's Architecture Repository that can be re-used in the architecture development. The specification of building blocks using the ADM is an evolutionary and iterative process.

See Section 5.5 for further information.

3.23 Solution Building Blocks

Solution Building Blocks (SBBs) relate to the Solutions Continuum. They are implementations of the architectures identified in the enterprise's Architecture Continuum and may be either procured or developed.

SBBs appear in Phase E of the ADM where product-specific building blocks are considered for the first time. SBBs define what products and components will implement the functionality, thereby defining the implementation. They fulfill business requirements and are product or vendor-aware. The content of an SBB specification includes the following as a minimum:

- Specific functionality and attributes
- Interfaces; the implemented set
- Required SBBs used with required functionality and names of the interfaces used

- Mapping from the SBBs to the IT topology and operational policies
- Specifications of attributes shared such as security, manageability, localizability, scalability
- Performance, configurability
- Design drivers and constraints, including the physical architecture
- Relationships between the SBBs and ABBs

3.24 Capability-Based Planning

Phases E and F feature a detailed method for defining and planning enterprise transformation based on the principles of capability-based planning, a business planning technique that focuses on business outcomes. It is business-driven and business-led and combines the requisite efforts of all lines of business to achieve the desired capability. It accommodates most, if not all, of the corporate business models and is especially useful in organizations where a latent capability to respond (e.g., an emergency preparedness unit) is required and the same resources are involved in multiple capabilities. Often the need for these capabilities is discovered and refined using business scenarios.

Figure 5 illustrates the relationship between capability-based planning, enterprise architecture, and portfolio/project management.

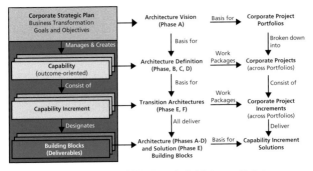

Figure 5: Relationship between Capabilities, Enterprise Architecture, and Projects

3.25 Migration Planning Techniques

A number of techniques are provided to support migration planning in Phases E and F. These are described in the following sections.

3.25.1 Implementation Factor Assessment and Deduction Matrix

The technique of creating an Implementation Factor Assessment and Deduction Matrix is used in Phase E to document factors having an impact on the architecture Implementation and Migration Plan. The matrix should include a list of the factors, their descriptions, and the deductions (conclusions) that indicate the actions or constraints that have to be taken into consideration when formulating the plans.

An example matrix is shown in Table 10.

Table 10: Implementation Factor Assessment and Deduction Matrix

Implementation Factor Assessment and Deduction Matrix		
Factor	Description	Deduction
<Name of the Factor>	<Description of the Factor>	<Impact on the Migration Plan>
Change in Technology	Shut down the message centers, saving 700 personnel, and have them replaced by email.	Need for personnel training, re-assignment Email has major personnel savings and should be given priority.
Consolidation of Services	…	…
Introduction of New Customer Service	…	…

3.25.2 Consolidated Gaps, Solutions, and Dependencies Matrix

The technique of creating a Consolidated Gaps, Solutions, and Dependencies Matrix allows the architect to group the gaps identified in the domain architecture gap analysis results and assess potential solutions and dependencies to one or more gaps. An example is shown in Table 11. This matrix can be used as a planning tool when creating work packages. The identified dependencies drive the creation of projects and migration planning in Phases E and F.

3.25.3 Architecture Definition Increments Table

The technique of creating an Architecture Definition Increments Table allows the architect to plan a series of Transition Architectures outlining the status of the enterprise architecture at specified times. A table should be drawn up, as shown in Table 12, listing the projects and then assigning their incremental deliverables across the Transition Architectures.

Table 11: Consolidated Gaps, Solutions, and Dependencies Matrix

Consolidated Gaps, Solutions, and Dependencies Matrix				
#	Architecture	Gap	Potential Solutions	Dependencies
1	Business	New Order Processing Process	Use COTS software tool process Implement custom solution	Drives Application #2
2	Application	New Order Processing Application	COTS software tool X Develop in-house	
3	Information	Consolidated Customer Information Base	Use COTS customer base Develop customer data mart	

Table 12: Example Architecture Definition Increments Table

Architecture Definition: Project Objectives by Increment				
	April 2007/2008	April 2008/2009	April 2009/2010	
Project	Transitional Architecture 1: Preparation	Transitional Architecture 2: Initial Operational Capability	Transitional Architecture 3: Benefits	Comments
Enterprise e-Services Capability	Training and Business Process	e-licensing capability	e-employment benefits	
IT e-Forms	Design and Build			
IT e-Information Environment	Design and Build Information Environment	Client Common Data Web Content Design and Build	Enterprise Common Data Document Management Design and Build	
…	…	…	…	…

3.25.4   Enterprise Architecture State Evolution Table

The technique of creating the Enterprise Architecture State Evolution Table allows the architect to show the proposed state of the architectures at various levels using the Technical Reference Model (TRM).

A table should be drawn, listing the services from the TRM used in the enterprise, the Transition Architectures, and proposed transformations, as shown in Table 13.

All Solution Building Blocks (SBBs) should be described with respect to their delivery and impact on these services. They should also be marked to show the progression of the enterprise architecture. In the example, where target capability has been reached, this is shown as "new" or "retain"; where capability is transitioned to a new solution, this is marked as "transition"; and where a capability is to be replaced, this is marked as "replace".

Table 13: Example Enterprise Architecture State Evolution Table

Architectural State Using the Technical Reference Model				
Sub-Domain	Service	Transition Architecture 1	Transition Architecture 2	Transition Architecture 3
Infrastructure Applications	Information Exchange Services	Solution System A (replace)	Solution System B-1 (transition)	Solution System B-2 (new)
	Data Management Services	Solution System D (retain)	Solution System D (retain)	Solution System D (retain)
…	…			

3.25.5 Business Value Assessment Technique

A technique to assess business value is to draw up a matrix based on a value index dimension and a risk index dimension. An example is shown in Figure 6. The value index should include criteria such as compliance to principles, financial contribution, strategic alignment, and competitive position. The risk index should include criteria such as size and complexity, technology, organizational capacity, and impact of a failure. Each criterion should be assigned an individual weight.

The index and its criteria and weighting should be developed and approved by senior management. It is important to establish the decision-making criteria before the options are known.

(Project size indicated by size of circle.)

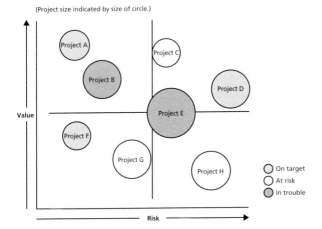

Figure 6: Business Value Assessment Matrix

3.26 Implementation and Migration Plan

The Implementation and Migration Plan is developed in Phases E and F, and provides a schedule for implementation of the solution described by a Transition Architecture. The Implementation and Migration Plan includes timing, cost, resources, benefits, and milestones for the implementation.

Typical contents are as follows:
- Implementation and Migration Strategy:
  - Strategic Implementation Direction
  - Implementation Sequencing Approach
- Interactions with other management frameworks:
  - Approach to aligning architecture and business planning
  - Approach to integration of architecture efforts
  - Approach to aligning architecture and portfolio/project management
  - Approach to aligning architecture and operations management

- Project charters:
  - Capabilities delivered by projects
  - Included work packages
  - Business value
  - Risk, issues, assumptions, dependencies
- Implementation plan:
  - Phase and workstream breakdown of implementation effort
  - Allocation of work packages to phase and workstream
  - Milestones and timing
  - Work breakdown structure
  - Resource requirements and costs

3.27 Transition Architecture

One ore more Transition Architectures are defined as outputs from Phase E. A Transition Architecture shows the enterprise at incremental states reflecting periods of transition that sit between the Baseline and Target Architectures. Transition Architectures are used to allow for individual work packages and projects to be grouped into managed portfolios and programs, illustrating the business value at each stage.

The following contents are typical within a Transition Architecture:
- Opportunity portfolio:
  - Consolidated gaps, solutions, and dependency assessment
  - Opportunity description
  - Benefit assessment
  - Capabilities and capability increments
  - Interoperability and co-existence requirements
- Work package portfolio:
  - Work package description (name, description, objectives, deliverables)
  - Functional requirements

– Dependencies
– Relationship to opportunity
– Relationship to Architecture Definition Document and Architecture Requirements Specification
• Milestone and milestone Transition Architectures:
– Definition of transition states
– Business Architecture for each transition state
– Data Architecture for each transition state
– Application Architecture for each transition state
– Technology Architecture for each transition state
• Implementation Factor Assessment and Deduction matrix, including:
– Risks
– Issues
– Assumptions
– Dependencies
– Actions
• Consolidated Gaps, Solutions, and Dependencies matrix, including:
– Architecture domain
– Gap
– Potential solutions
– Dependencies

3.28 Implementation Governance Model

Once an architecture has been defined, it is necessary to plan how the Transition Architecture that implements the architecture will be governed through implementation. Within organizations that have established architecture functions, there is likely to be a governance framework already in place, but specific processes, organizations, roles, responsibilities, and measures may need to be defined on a project-by-project basis.

The Implementation Governance Model produced as an output of Phase F ensures that a project transitioning into implementation also smoothly transitions into appropriate architecture governance (for Phase G).

Typical contents of an Implementation Governance Model are:
- Governance processes
- Governance organization structure
- Governance roles and responsibilities
- Governance checkpoints and success/failure criteria

3.29 Architecture Contracts

Architecture Contracts are produced in Phase G: Implementation Governance. Architecture Contracts are the joint agreements between development partners and sponsors on the deliverables, quality, and fitness-for-purpose of an architecture. Successful implementation of these agreements will be delivered through effective architecture. By implementing a governed approach to the management of contracts, the following will be ensured:
- A system of continuous monitoring to check integrity, changes, decision-making, and audit of all architecture-related activities within the organization
- Adherence to the principles, standards, and requirements of the existing or developing architectures
- Identification of risks in all aspects of the development and implementation of the architecture(s) covering the internal development against accepted standards, policies, technologies, and products as well as the operational aspects of the architectures such that the organization can continue its business within a resilient environment
- A set of processes and practices that ensure accountability, responsibility, and discipline with regard to the development and usage of all architectural artifacts

- A formal understanding of the governance organization responsible for the contract, their level of authority, and scope of the architecture under the governance of this body

TOGAF 9 identifies two example contracts as follows:
- Architecture Design and Development Contract
- Business Users' Architecture Contract

Typical contents of an Architecture Design and Development Contract are:
- Introduction and background
- The nature of the agreement
- Scope of the architecture
- Architecture and strategic principles and requirements
- Conformance requirements
- Architecture development and management process and roles
- Target Architecture measures
- Defined phases of deliverables
- Prioritized joint work plan
- Time window(s)
- Architecture delivery and business metrics

Typical contents of a Business Users' Architecture Contract produced in Phase G are:
- Introduction and background
- The nature of the agreement
- Scope
- Strategic requirements
- Conformance requirements
- Architecture adopters
- Time window
- Architecture business metrics
- Service architecture (includes Service Level Agreement (SLA))

This contract is also used to manage changes to the enterprise architecture in Phase H.

3.30 Change Request

Requests for Architecture Change are considered in Phase H: Architecture Change Management.

During implementation of an architecture, as more facts become known, it is possible that the original architecture definition and requirements are not suitable or are not sufficient to complete the implementation of a solution. In these circumstances, it is necessary for implementation projects to either deviate from the suggested architectural approach or to request scope extensions. Additionally, external factors – such as market factors, changes in business strategy, and new technology opportunities – may open up opportunities to extend and refine the architecture.

In these circumstances, a Change Request may be submitted in order to kick-start a further cycle of architecture work.

Typical contents of a Change Request are:
- Description of the proposed change
- Rationale for the proposed change
- Impact assessment of the proposed change, including:
  - Reference to specific requirements
  - Stakeholder priority of the requirements to date
  - Phases to be revisited
  - Phase to lead on requirements prioritization
  - Results of phase investigations and revised priorities
  - Recommendations on management of requirements
- Repository reference number

3.31 Compliance Assessment

Once an architecture has been defined, it is necessary to govern that architecture through implementation to ensure that the original Architecture Vision is appropriately realized and that any implementation lessons are fed back into the architecture process. Periodic compliance reviews of implementation projects in Phase G provide a mechanism to review project progress and ensure that the design and implementation is proceeding in-line with the strategic and architectural objectives.

Typical contents of a Compliance Assessment are:
- Overview of project progress and status
- Overview of project architecture/design
- Completed architecture checklists:
  - Hardware and operating system checklist
  - Software services and middleware checklist
  - Applications checklists
  - Information management checklists
  - Security checklists
  - System management checklists
  - System engineering checklists
  - Methods and tools checklists

3.32 Requirements Impact Assessment

Throughout the ADM, new information is collected relating to an architecture. As this information is gathered, new facts may come to light that invalidate existing aspects of the architecture. A Requirements Impact Assessment assesses the current architecture requirements and specification to identify changes that should be made and the implications of those changes.

It documents an assessment of the changes and the recommendations for change to the architecture. The recommended contents are as follows:

- Reference to specific requirements
- Stakeholder priority of the requirements to date
- Phases to be revisited
- Phase to lead on requirements prioritization
- Results of phase investigations and revised priorities
- Recommendations on management of requirements
- Repository reference number

These are often produced as a response to a Change Request.

Chapter 4
Guidelines for Adapting the ADM

This chapter provides guidelines for adapting the ADM.

4.1 Introduction

The ADM is a generic method for architecture development, which is designed to deal with most system and organizational requirements. However, it will often be necessary to modify or extend the ADM to suit specific needs. One of the tasks before applying the ADM is to review the process and its outputs for applicability, and then tailor them as appropriate to the circumstances of the individual enterprise. This activity may well produce an "enterprise-specific" ADM.

There are a number of reasons for wanting to tailor the ADM to the circumstances of an individual enterprise. Some of the reasons are outlined as follows:

1. An important consideration is that the order of the phases in the ADM is to some extent dependent on the maturity of the architecture discipline within the enterprise concerned. For example, if the business case for doing architecture is not well recognized, then creating an Architecture Vision is essential; and a detailed Business Architecture needs to come next to define the business case for the remaining architecture work, and secure the active participation of key stakeholders in that work.

2. The order of phases may also be defined by the business and architecture principles of an enterprise. For example, the business principles may dictate that the enterprise be prepared to adjust its business processes to meet the needs of a packaged solution, so that it can be implemented

quickly to enable fast response to market changes. In such a case, the Business Architecture (or at least the completion of it) may well follow completion of the Information Systems Architecture.

3. An enterprise may wish to use or tailor the ADM in conjunction with another enterprise architecture framework that has a defined set of deliverables specific to a particular vertical sector: Government, Defense, e-Business, Telecommunications, etc.

4. The ADM is one of many corporate processes that make up the corporate governance model for an enterprise. The ADM is complementary to, and supportive of, other standard program management processes. The enterprise will tailor the ADM to reflect the relationships with, and dependencies on, the other management processes.

5. The ADM is being mandated for use by a prime or lead contractor in an outsourcing situation, and needs to be tailored to achieve a suitable compromise between the contractor's existing practices and the contracting enterprise's requirements.

6. The enterprise is a small-to-medium enterprise, and wishes to use a "cut-down" version of the ADM that is more attuned to the reduced level of resources and system complexity typical of such an environment.

7. The enterprise is very large and complex, comprising many separate but interlinked "enterprises" within an overall collaborative business framework, and the architecture method needs to be adapted to recognize this. Such enterprises usually cannot be treated successfully as a single entity and a more federated approach is required.

The ADM process can also be adapted to deal with a number of different use scenarios, including different process styles (e.g., the use of iteration) and also specific specialist architectures (such as security). These are discussed in the following sections.

4.2   Applying Iteration to the ADM

The ADM supports a number of concepts that could be characterized as iteration. It is expected that:

- Project teams will iterate through the entire ADM cycle, commencing new vision activity as a result of Architecture Change Management.
- Project teams may cycle between ADM phases, in planned cycles covering multiple phases (e.g., Business Architecture, Information Systems Architecture, and Technology Architecture).
- Project teams may return to previous phases in order to circle back and update work products with new information.
- Many project teams may operate their own ADM cycles concurrently, with relationships between different teams. For example, one architecture team may trigger a request for work for another architecture team.

All of these techniques are valid applications of the ADM and can be used to ensure that the approach to architecture development is sufficiently flexible to accommodate other methods and frameworks.

TOGAF 9 includes consideration of the organizational factors that influence the extent to which the ADM should be used in an iterative fashion, different styles of iteration, and a mapping of ADM phases to iteration cycles for architecture definition.

A suggested iteration cycle for iterations that span multiple ADM phases is shown in Figure 7.

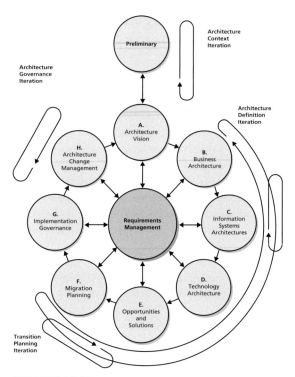

Figure 7: Iteration Cycles

- **Architecture Context** iterations allow initial mobilization of the architecture activity by establishing the approach, principles, and scope.
- **Architecture Definition** iterations allow creation of content by cycling through the Business, Information Systems, and Technology Architecture phases.
- **Transition Planning** iterations support the creation of formal change roadmaps.
- **Architecture Governance** iterations support governance of change activity progressing towards a defined Target Architecture.

TOGAF 9 defines two styles of architecture definition:
- **Baseline First**: In this style, the Baseline Architecture is assessed first. This process is suitable when a target solution is not clearly understood.
- **Target First**: In this style, the Target Architecture is elaborated in detail and then mapped back to the baseline, in order to define change activity. This process is suitable when a target state is agreed to at a high level and the enterprise wishes to avoid proliferating current business practice into the target.

TOGAF 9 maps both styles to iteration cycles, as illustrated in Figure 8 and Figure 9.

TOGAF Phase		Architecture Context	Architecture Definition			Transition Planning		Architecture Governance	
		Initial Iteration	Iteration 1	Iteration 2	Iteration n	Iteration 1	Iteration n	Iteration 1	Iteration n
Preliminary		Core	Informal	Informal	Informal				Light
Architecture Vision		Core	Informal	Informal	Informal	Informal	Informal		Light
Business Architecture	Baseline	Informal	Core	Light	Core	Informal	Informal		Light
	Target	Informal	Informal	Core	Core	Informal	Informal		Light
Application Architecture	Baseline	Informal	Core	Light	Core	Informal	Informal		Light
	Target	Informal	Informal	Core	Core	Informal	Informal		Light
Data Architecture	Baseline	Informal	Core	Light	Core	Informal	Informal		Light
	Target	Informal	Informal	Core	Core	Informal	Informal		Light
Technology Architecture	Baseline	Informal	Core	Light	Core	Informal	Informal		Light
	Target	Informal	Informal	Core	Core	Informal	Informal		Light
Opportunities and Solutions		Informal	Light	Light	Light	Core	Core	Informal	Informal
Migration Planning		Informal	Light	Light	Light	Core	Core	Informal	Informal
Implementation Governance						Informal	Informal	Core	Core
Change Management			Informal	Informal	Informal	Informal	Informal	Core	Core

Core: primary focus activity for the iteration

Light: secondary focus activity for the iteration

Informal: potential activity for the iteration, not formally mentioned in the method

Figure 8: Activity by Iteration for Baseline First Architecture Definition

TOGAF Phase		Architecture Context	Architecture Definition			Transition Planning		Architecture Governance	
		Initial Iteration	Iteration 1	Iteration 2	Iteration n	Iteration 1	Iteration n	Iteration 1	Iteration n
Preliminary		Core	Informal	Informal	Informal				Light
Architecture Vision		Core	Informal	Informal	Informal	Informal	Informal		Light
Business Architecture	Baseline	Informal	Core	Core	Core	Informal	Informal		Light
	Target	Informal	Core	Light	Core	Informal	Informal		Light
Application Architecture	Baseline	Informal	Informal	Core	Core	Informal	Informal		Light
	Target	Informal	Core	Light	Core	Informal	Informal		Light
Data Architecture	Baseline	Informal	Informal	Core	Core	Informal	Informal		Light
	Target	Informal	Core	Light	Core	Informal	Informal		Light
Technology Architecture	Baseline	Informal	Informal	Core	Core	Informal	Informal		Light
	Target	Informal	Core	Light	Core	Informal	Informal		Light
Opportunities and Solutions		Informal	Light	Light	Light	Core	Core	Informal	Informal
Migration Planning		Informal	Light	Light	Light	Core	Core	Informal	Informal
Implementation Governance						Informal	Informal	Core	Core
Change Management			Informal	Informal	Informal	Informal	Informal	Core	Core

Core: primary focus activity for the iteration

Light: secondary focus activity for the iteration

Informal: potential activity for the iteration, not formally mentioned in the method

Figure 9: Activity by Iteration for Target First Architecture Definition

4.3 Applying the ADM at Different Enterprise Levels

The ADM is intended to be used as a model to support the definition and implementation of architecture at multiple levels within an enterprise. As it is not possible to develop a single architecture that addresses all the needs of all stakeholders, the enterprise must be partitioned into different areas, each of which can be supported by architectures. Enterprise architectures are typically partitioned according to Subject Matter, Time Period, and Level of Detail, as illustrated in Figure 10.

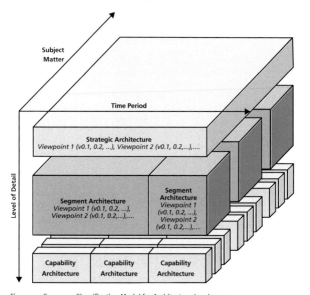

Figure 10: Summary Classification Model for Architecture Landscape

TOGAF 9 describes the types of engagement that architects may be required to perform and how the ADM can be used to coordinate activities of various teams of architects working at different levels. It also provides two strategies for using the ADM as a process to support hierarchies of architectures:

• Architectures at different levels can be developed through iterations within a single ADM process. Using this approach, as illustrated in Figure 11, the Architecture Vision phase can be used to develop a strategic view of the architecture. Phases B, C, and D then provide a more detailed and formal architectural view of the landscape for different segments or time periods. Phases E and F then develop a detailed Migration Plan, which may include even more detailed and specific Capability Architectures.

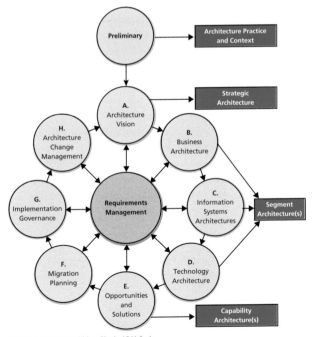

Figure 11: Iterations within a Single ADM Cycle

- In cases where larger-scale architectures need to be developed by a number of different architecture teams, a more hierarchical application of the ADM may be used. This approach to the ADM uses the Migration Planning phase of one ADM cycle to initiate new projects, which will also develop architectures. Architectures at different levels can be developed through a hierarchy of ADM processes, executed concurrently as shown in Figure 12.

4.4   Security Architecture and the ADM

TOGAF 9 provides guidance on the security considerations that need to be addressed during application of the ADM. It helps the enterprise architect deploying the ADM to inform the security architect of what security architectural changes must be effected. It is also intended as a guide to help the enterprise architect avoid missing a critical security concern.

All groups of stakeholders in an enterprise will have security concerns, which might not be immediately visible as such unless the architect is cognizant of their nature. It is recommended to bring a security architect into the project as early as possible. Throughout the phases of the ADM, guidance is offered on security-specific information which should be gathered, steps which should be taken, and artifacts which should be created. Architecture decisions related to security, like all others, should be traceable to business and policy decisions, which should derive from a risk analysis. The generally accepted areas of concern for the security architect are:

- Authentication: The substantiation of the identity of a person or entity related to the system in some way.
- Authorization: The definition and enforcement of permitted capabilities for a person or entity whose identity has been established.
- Audit: The ability to provide forensic data attesting that the system was used in accordance with stated security policies.

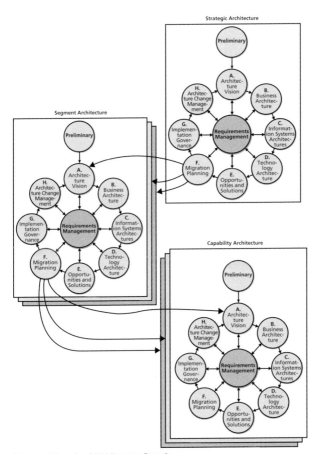

Figure 12: A Hierarchy of ADM Processes Example

- Assurance: The ability to test and prove that the system has the security attributes required to uphold the stated security policies.
- Availability: The ability of the system to function without service interruption or depletion despite abnormal or malicious events.
- Asset Protection: The protection of information assets from loss or unintended disclosure, and resources from unauthorized and unintended use.
- Administration: The ability to add and change security policies, add or change how policies are implemented in the system, and add or change the persons or entities related to the system.
- Risk Management: The organization's attitude to and tolerance for risk.

Typical security architecture artifacts would include:
- Business rules regarding handling of data/information assets
- Written and published security policy
- Codified data/information asset ownership and custody
- Risk analysis documentation
- Data classification policy documentation

4.5   Using TOGAF to Define and Govern SOAs

TOGAF 9 describes Service Oriented Architecture (SOA) as an architectural style, how enterprise architecture supports SOA, the correspondence between SOA and TOGAF terminology, and provides guidance on defining a service contract definition.

SOA, as an architectural style, tries to simplify the business, and the interoperation of its parts, by structuring capability as well-defined granular services as opposed to opaque, silo'ed business units. It permits identification of functional capabilities of an organization, and thus an opportunity to reduce duplication. By standardizing behavior and interoperation of services, it is possible to limit the impacts of change and also to plan for the impact of future changes.

Enterprise architecture discipline provides the following tools and techniques to assist organizations with SOAs:

- Enterprise architecture defines structured traceable representations of business and technology that link IT assets to the business they support in a clear and measurable way. These models in turn support impact assessment and portfolio management against a much richer context.
- Enterprise architecture defines principles, constraints, frameworks, patterns, and standards that form the basis of design governance, ensuring aligned services, interoperability, and re-use.
- Enterprise architecture links many different perspectives to a single business problem (business, data, application, technology, abstracted, concrete, etc.) providing a consistent model to address various problem domains and extensive test for completeness.
- Enterprise architecture provides consistent abstractions of high-level strategies and project deliverables, enabling both bottom-up and top-down outputs to be collated in a shared repository to support planning and analysis.

Using these techniques, enterprise architecture becomes a foundation for deployment of an SOA approach within an organization, because:

- It links SOA stakeholders together, ensuring that the needs of each stakeholder community are met and that each stakeholder community is aware of appropriate context.
- It provides a link from business to IT that can be used to justify the cost of IT re-engineering against business value.
- It shows which services should be built and how they should be re-used.
- It shows how services should be designed and how platforms must interoperate.
- It provides a repository to hold and maintain design-related information on an ongoing basis.

TOGAF has a number of concepts in the TOGAF content metamodel (see Chapter 5) that support the modeling of SOA concepts:

- Function: A function is a thing that a business does. Services support functions, are functions, and have functions, but functions are not necessarily services. Services have more specific constraints than functions.
- Business Service: A business service is a thing that a business does that has a defined, measured interface and has contracts with consumers of the service. A business service is supported by combinations of people, process, and technology.
- Information System Service: An information system service is a thing that a business does that has a defined, measured interface and has contracts with consumers of the service. Information system services are directly supported by applications and have associations to SOA service interfaces.
- Application Component: An application component is a configured and deployed system, or an independently governed part of a configured and deployed system. Application components provide information system services. Application components can be physical applications and also logical applications that group together applications of a similar type.
- Technology Component: A technology component is a piece of software or hardware that can be purchased from an internal or external supplier. Technology components are configured, combined, built on, and deployed in order to produce application components.

These are summarized in Figure 13.

4.5.1 Further Reading

The Open Group SOA Working Group is currently working to develop a Practical Guide that will enable a certified TOGAF practitioner to use TOGAF to develop an SOA. More information on the SOA Working Group and its projects can be found at www.opengroup.org/projects/soa.

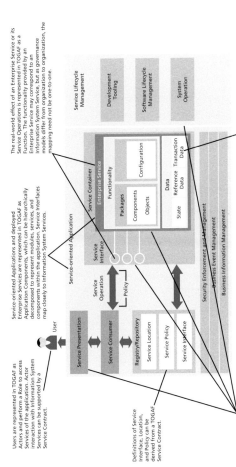

Users are represented in TOGAF as Actors and perform a Role to access Services of the application. Actor interaction with Information System Services can be supported by a Service Contract.

Service-oriented Applications and deployed Enterprise Services are represented in TOGAF as Application Components, which can be hierarchically decomposed to represent modules, services, and components within the application. Service Interfaces map closely to Information System Services.

The real-world effect of an Enterprise Service or its Service Operations is represented in TOGAF as a Function. The functionality provided by an Enterprise Service may correspond to an Information System Service, but as governance models differ from organization to organization, the mapping need not be one-to-one.

Definitions of Service Interface, Location, and Policy can be derived from a TOGAF Service Contract.

Products purchased to create a Service-oriented Application, such as COTS packages, purchased Enterprise Services, Service Container software, Registry software, Repository software, Lifecycle Management software, Database Management software, Security software Business Event Management software, Service Presentation software, and underlying hardware are represented in TOGAF as Technology Components.

Data encapsulated within an Enterprise Service can be represented in TOGAF using Data Entities that show the content of data and Information Components that show how data is encapsulated.

Figure 13: TOGAF Concepts Mapped to SOA Terminology

Chapter 5
Architecture Content Framework

This chapter provides an introduction to the Architecture Content Framework, a structured metamodel for architectural artifacts.

5.1 Architecture Content Framework Overview

During the execution of the ADM a number of outputs will be produced as a result, such as process flows, architectural requirements, project plans, project compliance assessments, etc. In order to be able to collate and present these major work products in a consistent and structured manner, it is necessary to have an Architecture Content Framework within which to place them. This allows for easier reference and standard classification, and also to help facilitate the structuring of relationships between the various constituent work products that make up what is often referred to as the "Enterprise Architecture".

The Architecture Content Framework provided in TOGAF 9 allows TOGAF to be used as a stand-alone framework for architecture within an enterprise. However, other content frameworks exist (such as ArchiMate and the Zachman Framework) and it is expected that some enterprises may opt to use an external framework in conjunction with the ADM instead. In these cases, the TOGAF Architecture Content Framework provides a useful reference and starting point for TOGAF content to be mapped to the metamodels of other frameworks.

In order to assist with the classification of new work products and the potential need to correlate with other content frameworks (including any existing classified architecture work products), the Architecture Content

Framework uses the following three categories to describe the type of architectural work product within its context of use:

- A **deliverable** is a formal work product that is contractually specified, and would normally be reviewed, agreed, and signed off by its stakeholders. Deliverables often represent the output of projects.
- An **artifact** is a more granular architectural work product that describes an architecture from a specific viewpoint. This would include such things as a use-case specification, a list of architectural requirements, or a network diagram. Artifacts are generally classified as either catalogs (lists of things), matrices (showing relationships between things), or diagrams (pictures of things). An architectural deliverable may contain many artifacts.
- A **building block** represents a (potentially re-usable) component of business, IT, or architectural capability that can be combined with other building blocks to deliver architectures and solutions.

Building blocks can be defined at various levels of detail and can relate to both "architectures" and "solutions", with Architecture Building Blocks (ABBs) typically describing the required capability in order to shape the Solution Building Blocks (SBBs) which would represent the components to be used to implement the required capability. These are discussed further in Section 5.5.

The relationships between deliverables, artifacts, and building blocks are shown in Figure 14.

5.2   Content Metamodel

The Architecture Content Framework is based upon a standard content metamodel which provides a definition for all the types of building blocks that exist within an architecture. A high-level overview of the content metamodel is shown in Figure 15. The metamodel illustrates how these building blocks can be described and how they relate to one another.

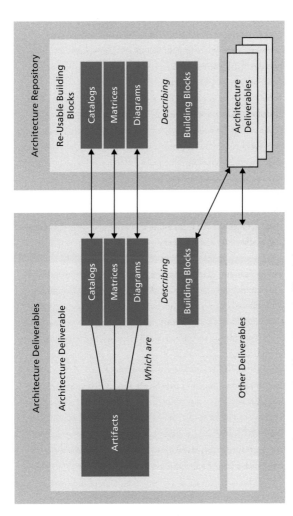

Figure 14: Relationships between Deliverables, Artifacts, and Building Blocks

When creating and managing architectures, it is necessary to consider various concerns such as business services, actors, applications, data entities, and technology. The content metamodel highlights these concerns, shows their relationships, and identifies artifacts that can be used to represent them in a consistent, structured manner.

Additionally, the content metamodel can be used to provide guidance to any organizations that wish to implement their architecture using an architecture tool.

5.2.1 Core and Extensions

The model has been structured to consider core and extension content, where the core metamodel provides a minimum set of architectural content that supports traceability across artifacts, and extensions are plugged in to support any more specific or in-depth modeling that may be required.

Extensions are logically clustered into catalogs, matrices, and diagrams, allowing focus in areas of specific interest. All extension modules are optional and should be selected during the Preliminary phase of the ADM iteration to meet the needs of the organization. The extensions described in TOGAF are for guidance and can be added to or tailored accordingly.

5.2.2 Catalogs, Matrices, and Diagrams

Whilst the content metamodel is used to support the structuring of architectural information, most stakeholders do not need or wish to know the detail contained within the Architecture Content Framework in this manner. Therefore, the use of catalogs, matrices, and diagrams is introduced to facilitate the presentation of architectural information so that it may be used for reference and governance purposes more readily.

Catalogs are lists of building blocks of a specific type or related types, matrices are grids that show relationships between two or more entities, and diagrams are graphical renderings of architectural content.

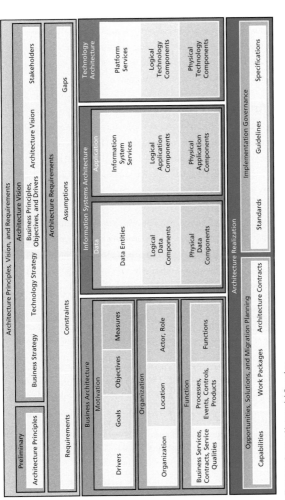

Figure 15: Content Metamodel Overview

In summary, the results of an ADM developed architecture consists of a number of defined ABBs populated into architecture catalogs, with relationships specified between those building blocks in architecture matrices, and then presented as communication diagrams that show in a precise and concise way what the architecture is.

5.3   Architectural Artifacts

TOGAF 9 describes a set of atomic work products that are created when developing an architecture by following the ADM. These work products are labeled as artifacts and represent an individual model of a system, solution, or enterprise state, which could potentially be re-used in a variety of contexts.

An artifact is distinct from a deliverable, which is a contracted output from a project. In most cases, deliverables will contain artifacts and each artifact may exist in many deliverables. The basic concepts and terminology used in this section have been adapted from ISO/IEC 42010:2007, described in Table 14 and illustrated in Figure 16.[6]

Table 14: Concepts Related to Architecture Views

Concept	Definition
System	A system is a collection of components organized to accomplish a specific function or set of functions.
Architecture	The architecture of a system is the system's fundamental organization, embodied in its components, their relationships to each other and to the environment, and the principles guiding its design and evolution.
Architectural Description	An architectural description is a collection of artifacts that document an architecture. In TOGAF, architecture views are the key artifacts in an architecture description.

---

6 Reprinted with permission from IEEE Std 1471-2000, Systems and Software Engineering – Recommended Practice for Architectural Description of Software-intensive Systems, Copyright © 2000, by IEEE. The IEEE disclaims any responsibility resulting from the placement and use in the described manner.

Concept	Definition
Stakeholders	Stakeholders are people who have key roles in, or concerns about, the system; for example, as users, developers, or managers. Different stakeholders with different roles in the system will have different concerns. Stakeholders can be individuals, teams, or organizations (or classes thereof).
Concerns	Concerns are the key interests that are crucially important to the stakeholders in the system, and determine the acceptability of the system. Concerns may pertain to any aspect of the system's functioning, development, or operation, including considerations such as performance, reliability, security, distribution, and evolvability.
View	A view is a representation of a whole system from the perspective of a related set of concerns. In capturing or representing the design of a system's architecture, the architect will typically create one or more architecture models, possibly using different tools. A view will comprise selected parts of one or more models, chosen so as to demonstrate to a particular stakeholder or group of stakeholders that their concerns are being adequately addressed in the design of the system architecture.
Viewpoint	A viewpoint defines the perspective from which a view is taken. More specifically, a viewpoint defines: how to construct and use a view (by means of an appropriate schema or template); the information that should appear in the view; the modeling techniques for expressing and analyzing the information; and a rationale for these choices (e.g., by describing the purpose and intended audience of the view).

TOGAF 9 provides a set of example architecture viewpoints, summarized in Table 15, that may be adopted, enhanced, and combined to produce views describing an architecture.

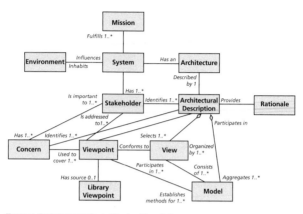

Figure 16: Basic Concepts for Architectural Description

Table 15: Example Viewpoints by ADM Phase

ADM Phase	Viewpoint
Viewpoints in the Preliminary Phase	Principles catalog
Viewpoints in Phase A	Stakeholder Map matrix Value Chain diagram Solution Concept diagram
Viewpoints in Phase B	Organization/Actor catalog Driver/Goal/Objective catalog Role catalog Business Service/Function catalog Location catalog Process/Event/Control/Product catalog Contract/Measure catalog Business Interaction matrix Actor/Role matrix Business Footprint diagram Business Service/Information diagram Functional Decomposition diagram Product Lifecycle diagram Goal/Objective/Service diagram Use-Case diagram Organization Decomposition diagram Process Flow diagram Event diagram

ADM Phase	Viewpoint
Viewpoints in Phase C, Data Architecture	Data Entity/Data Component catalog Data Entity/Business Function matrix System/Data matrix Class diagram Data Dissemination diagram Data Security diagram Class Hierarchy diagram Data Migration diagram Data Lifecycle diagram
Viewpoints in Phase C, Application Architecture	Application Portfolio catalog Interface catalog System/Organization matrix Role/System matrix System/Function matrix Application Interaction matrix Application Communication diagram Application and User Location diagram System Use-Case diagram Enterprise Manageability diagram Process/System Realization diagram Software Engineering diagram Application Migration diagram Software Distribution diagram
Viewpoints in Phase D	Technology Standards catalog Technology Portfolio catalog System/Technology matrix Environments and Locations diagram Platform Decomposition diagram Processing diagram Networked Computing/Hardware diagram Communications Engineering diagram
Viewpoints in Phase E	Project Context diagram Benefits diagram
Viewpoints for Requirements Management	Requirements catalog

5.4 Architecture Deliverables

TOGAF 9, Part IV, Chapter 36 provides a typical baseline of architecture deliverables in order to better define the activities required in the ADM and act as a starting point for tailoring within an organization. For details, see Chapter 3.

5.5 Building Blocks

The Architecture Content Framework explains the concept of building blocks together with a fictional example illustrating building blocks in architecture. TOGAF includes Architecture Building Blocks (ABBs) and Solution Building Blocks (SBBs).

"Building blocks" is a pervasive term within TOGAF and the ADM. A building block is simply a package of functionality defined to meet business needs. The way in which functionality, products, and custom developments are assembled into building blocks will vary widely between individual architectures. Every organization must decide for itself what arrangement of building blocks works best. A good choice of building blocks can lead to improvements in legacy system integration, interoperability, and flexibility in the creation of new systems and applications.

Systems are built up from collections of building blocks, so most building blocks have to interoperate with other building blocks. Wherever that is true, it is important that the interfaces to a building block are published and reasonably stable.

Building blocks can be defined at various levels of detail, depending on what stage of architecture development has been reached.

For instance, at an early stage, a building block can simply consist of a grouping of functionality, such as a customer database and some retrieval tools. Building blocks at this functional level of definition are described in TOGAF as Architecture Building Blocks (ABBs); see Section 3.22. Later on, real products or custom developments replace these simple definitions of functionality, and the building blocks are then described as Solution Building Blocks (SBBs); see Section 3.23.

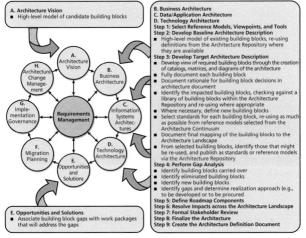

A. Architecture Vision
- High-level model of candidate building blocks

B. Business Architecture
C. Data/Application Architecture
D. Technology Architecture
Step 1: Select Reference Models, Viewpoints, and Tools
Step 2: Develop Baseline Architecture Description
- High-level model of existing building blocks, re-using definitions from the Architecture Repository where they are available
Step 3: Develop Target Architecture Description
- Develop view of required building blocks through the creation of catalogs, matrices, and diagrams of the architecture
- Fully document each building block
- Document rationale for building block decisions in architecture document
- Identify the impacted building blocks, checking against a library of building blocks within the Architecture Repository and re-using where appropriate
- Where necessary, define new building blocks
- Select standards for each building block, re-using as much as possible from reference models selected from the Architecture Continuum
- Document final mapping of the building blocks to the Architecture Landscape
- From selected building blocks, identify those that might be re-used, and publish as standards or reference models via the Architecture Repository
Step 4: Perform Gap Analysis
- Identify building blocks carried over
- Identify eliminated building blocks
- Identify new building blocks
- Identify gaps and determine realization approach (e.g., to be developed or to be procured
Step 5: Define Roadmap Components
Step 6: Resolve Impacts across the Architecture Landscape
Step 7: Formal Stakeholder Review
Step 8: Finalize the Architecture
Step 9: Create the Architecture Definition Document

E. Opportunities and Solutions
- Associate building block gaps with work packages that will address the gaps

Figure 17: Architecture Building Blocks and their Use in the ADM Cycle

The key phases and steps of the ADM at which building blocks are evolved and specified are summarized as follows, and illustrated in Figure 17.

In Phase A, the earliest building block definitions start as relatively abstract entities within the Architecture Vision.

In Phases B, C, and D building blocks within the Business, Data, Application, and Technology Architectures are evolved to a common pattern of steps.

Finally, in Phase E the building blocks become more implementation-specific as SBBs are identified to address gaps.

Chapter 6
The Enterprise Continuum

This chapter provides an introduction to the Enterprise Continuum. Topics addressed in this chapter include:

- An explanation of the Enterprise Continuum and its purpose
- Using the Enterprise Continuum in developing an enterprise architecture
- An overview of characteristics to classify and partition architectures
- An overview of a structural framework for an Architecture Repository

6.1 Overview of the Enterprise Continuum

The Enterprise Continuum, shown in Figure 18, provides a model for structuring a "virtual" repository that can be filled with architecture assets and their possible solutions (models, patterns, architecture descriptions, etc.). These assets and solutions can be drawn from within the enterprise or from the industry at large and used in constructing architectures.

A distinction is made between architectures and their possible solutions, thus creating an Architecture Continuum and a Solutions Continuum. As shown in Figure 18, the relationship between them is one of guidance and support.

The Enterprise Continuum supports two general ideas: re-use where possible, especially the avoidance of re-invention, and an aid to communication. The assets in both the Architecture and Solutions Continuums are structured from generic to specific in order to provide a consistent language to effectively communicate the differences between architectures. Understanding where you are in the continuum helps everyone to communicate effectively. Use of the Enterprise Continuum can eliminate ambiguity when discussing concepts and items amongst different

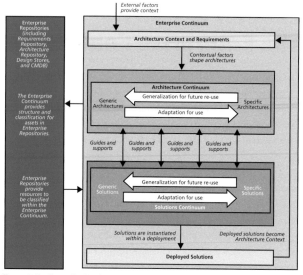

Figure 18: The Enterprise Continuum

departments within the same organization or even different organizations building enterprise architectures. Understanding the architecture helps to better understand the solution. Being able to explain the general concept behind a solution makes it easier to understand possible conflicts.

Since the use of the Enterprise Continuum is usually accompanied by an increase of associated architecture and solution assets, organizations can directly benefit from re-use.

6.1.1 The Enterprise Continuum and Architecture Re-Use

Examples of assets "within the enterprise" are the deliverables of previous architecture work, which are available for re-use. Examples of assets "in the IT industry at large" are the wide variety of industry reference models and architecture patterns that exist, and are continually emerging, including those that are highly generic (such as the TOGAF Technical Reference Model (TRM)); those specific to certain aspects of IT (such as a web services architecture); those specific to certain types of information processing (such as e-Commerce); and those specific to certain vertical industries (such as the ARTS data model from the retail industry). The decision as to which architecture assets a specific enterprise considers part of its own Enterprise Continuum will normally form part of the overall architecture governance function within the enterprise concerned.

6.1.2 Using the Enterprise Continuum within the ADM

In the ADM a process of moving from the TOGAF Foundation Architecture to an organization-specific architecture (or set of architectures) is described. This Foundation Architecture is a highly general description of generic services and functions that provide the foundation on which specific architectures and Architecture Building Blocks (ABBs) can be built by adding relevant architecture assets, components, and building blocks from the Enterprise Continuum. At relevant places throughout the ADM, there are reminders to consider which architecture assets the architect should use. In addition to the TOGAF Foundation Architecture, TOGAF provides another reference model for consideration for inclusion in an organization's Enterprise Continuum: the Integrated Information Infrastructure Reference Model (III-RM).

6.2   Architecture Partitioning

In a typical enterprise, multiple architectures will be in existence at any point in time. Some architectures will address specific needs; others will be more general. Some will address detail; some will provide an overview. Likewise, there will also be many solutions in use, or being considered for use, to meet the needs of the enterprise.

This leads to the need to partition architectures because:

- Addressing all problems within a single architecture is too complex.
- Different architectures conflict with one another (e.g., the state of the enterprise changes over time and an architecture from one time period will conflict with an architecture for a different time period).
- Different people need to work on different elements of architecture at the same time and partitions allow for specific groups of architects to own and develop specific segments of the architecture.
- Effective architecture re-use requires modular architecture segments that can be taken and incorporated into broader architectures and solutions.

One way of partitioning architecture is to use the scope or subject matter that the architecture addresses as a guideline, as indicated in Section 4.3. Another characteristic that can be considered for partitioning is the viewpoint or kind of architecture that can be broadly classified as business, data, application, and technology, as indicated in Section 1.4.

Architectures that describe particular solution approaches, best practices, or patterns can be developed (or acquired) and shared across the enterprise as reference models. Classification of these reference models can also assist with architecture partitioning. Figure 19 shows a model to classify reference models and associated architectures based on their level of abstraction or relevance to a specific organization.

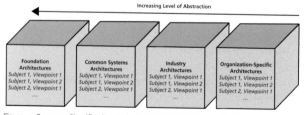

Figure 19: Summary Classification Model for Architecture Reference Models

6.3   Architecture Repository

Supporting the Enterprise Continuum is the concept of an Architecture Repository which can be used to store different classes of architectural output at different levels of abstraction, created by the ADM. In this way, TOGAF facilitates understanding and co-operation between stakeholders and practitioners at different levels.

By means of the Enterprise Continuum and Architecture Repository, architects are encouraged to leverage all other relevant architectural resources when developing an Organization-Specific Architecture.

In this context, the ADM can be regarded as describing a process lifecycle that operates at multiple levels within the organization, operating within a holistic governance framework and producing aligned outputs that reside in an Architecture Repository. The Enterprise Continuum provides a valuable context for understanding architectural models: it shows building blocks and their relationships to each other, and the constraints and requirements on a cycle of architecture development.

The structure of the TOGAF Architecture Repository is shown in Figure 20.

The major components within an Architecture Repository are as follows:
- The **Architecture Metamodel** describes the organizationally tailored application of an architecture framework, including a metamodel for architecture content.
- The **Architecture Capability** defines the parameters, structures, and processes that support governance of the Architecture Repository.
- The **Architecture Landscape** shows an architectural view of the building blocks that are in use within the organization today (e.g., a list of the live applications). The landscape is likely to exist at multiple levels of abstraction to suit different architecture objectives.

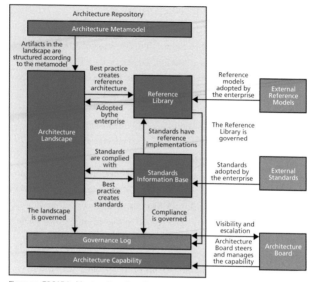

Figure 20: TOGAF Architecture Repository Structure

- The **Standards Information Base** (SIB) captures the standards with which new architectures must comply, which may include industry standards, selected products and services from suppliers, or shared services already deployed within the organization.
- The **Reference Library** provides guidelines, templates, patterns, and other forms of reference material that can be leveraged in order to accelerate the creation of new architectures for the enterprise.
- The **Governance Log** provides a record of governance activity across the enterprise.

Chapter 7
TOGAF Reference Models

This chapter provides a brief introduction to the TOGAF Reference Models.

7.1 TOGAF Foundation Architecture

The TOGAF Foundation Architecture is an architecture that provides a foundation on which specific architectures and architectural components can be built. This Foundation Architecture is embodied in the Technical Reference Model (TRM). The TRM is universally applicable and therefore can be used to build any system architecture.

7.1.1 Technical Reference Model (TRM)

The TRM, shown in Figure 21, is a model and taxonomy of generic platform services. The taxonomy defines the terminology and provides a coherent description of its components. Its purpose is to give a conceptual description of an Information System. And the TRM model is a graphical representation of the taxonomy to act as an aid for understanding.

7.2 Integrated Information Infrastructure Reference Model (III-RM)

Whereas the Foundation Architecture describes a typical application platform environment, the second reference model included in the Enterprise Continuum, the Integrated Information Infrastructure Reference Model (III-RM), focuses on the application software space. The III-RM is a "Common Systems Architecture" in Enterprise Continuum terms.

The III-RM is shown in Figure 22 and is a subset of the TOGAF TRM in terms of its overall scope, but it also expands certain parts of the TRM, in particular in the business applications and infrastructure applications parts.

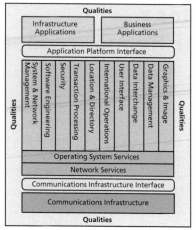

Figure 21: Technical Reference Model (TRM)

The III-RM provides help in addressing one of the key challenges facing the enterprise architect today: the need to design an integrated information infrastructure to enable Boundaryless Information Flow.

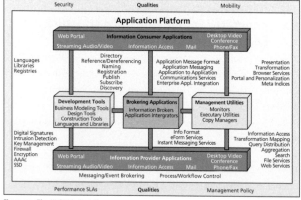

Figure 22: The III-RM in Detail

Chapter 8
Architecture Capability Framework

This chapter introduces the Architecture Capability Framework.

TOGAF 9, Part VII: Architecture Capability Framework provides a set of reference materials for how to establish such an architecture function.

A summary of the contents of TOGAF 9, Part VII is shown in Table 16. An overall structure for an Architecture Capability Framework is shown in Figure 23.

Table 16: TOGAF 9 Part VII Contents Summary

Chapter	Description
Establishing an Architecture Capability	Guidelines for establishing an Architecture Capability within an organization.
Architecture Board	Guidelines for establishing and operating an enterprise Architecture Board.
Architecture Compliance	Guidelines for ensuring project compliance to architecture.
Architecture Contracts	Guidelines for defining and using Architecture Contracts.
Architecture Governance	Framework and guidelines for architecture governance.
Architecture Maturity Models	Techniques for evaluating and quantifying an organization's maturity in enterprise architecture.
Architecture Skills Framework	A set of role, skill, and experience norms for staff undertaking enterprise architecture work.

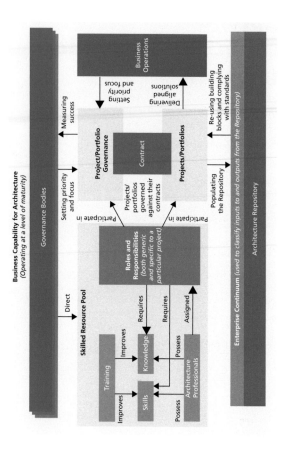

Figure 23: Architecture Capability Framework

8.1 Establishing an Architecture Capability

Implementing any capability within an organization requires the design of the four domain architectures: Business, Data, Application, and Technology. Establishing the architecture practice within an organization therefore requires the design of:

- The Business Architecture of the architecture practice, which highlights the architecture governance, architecture processes, architecture organizational structure, architecture information requirements, architecture products, etc.
- The Data Architecture, which defines the structure of the organization's Enterprise Continuum and Architecture Repository
- The Application Architecture, which specifies the functionality and/or applications services required to enable the architecture practice
- The Technology Architecture, which specifies the architecture practice's infrastructure requirements in support of the architecture applications and Enterprise Continuum.

8.2 Architecture Governance

The Architecture Capability Framework contains a framework and guidelines for architecture governance. Architecture governance is the practice by which enterprise architectures and other architectures are managed and controlled at an enterprise-wide level. It includes the following:

- Implementing a system of controls over the creation and monitoring of all architecture components and activities, to ensure the effective introduction, implementation, and evolution of architectures within the organization
- Implementing a system to ensure compliance with internal and external standards and regulatory obligations
- Establishing processes that support effective management of the above processes within agreed parameters

- Establishing and documenting decision structures that influence the enterprise architecture; this includes stakeholders that provide input to decisions
- Developing practices that ensure accountability to a clearly identified stakeholder community, both inside and outside the organization

8.3 Architecture Board

An enterprise architecture is more than just the artifacts produced by the application of the ADM process. Making the organization act according to the principles laid down in the architecture requires a decision-making framework. The Architecture Capability Framework provides a set of guidelines for establishing and operating an enterprise Architecture Board. An Architecture Board is responsible for operational items and must be capable of making decisions in situations of possible conflict and be accountable for taking those decisions. It should therefore be a representation of all the key stakeholders in the architecture, and will typically comprise a group of executives responsible for the review and maintenance of the overall architecture. It is important that the members of the Architecture Board cover architecture, business, and program management areas.

Issues for which the Architecture Board can be made responsible and accountable are:
- Consistency between sub-architectures
- Identifying re-usable components
- Flexibility of enterprise architecture; to meet business needs and utilize new technologies
- Enforcement of architecture compliance
- Improving the maturity level of architecture discipline within the organization
- Ensuring that the discipline of architecture-based development is adopted

- Providing the basis for all decision-making with regard to changes to the architectures
- Supporting a visible escalation capability for out-of-bounds decisions

The Architecture Board is also responsible for operational items, such as the monitoring and control of Architecture Contracts (see Section 3.29), and for governance items, such as producing usable governance materials. Important tasks are:

- Assigning architectural tasks
- Formally approving architectural products
- Resolving architectural conflicts

8.4 Architecture Compliance

Using architecture to structure IT development in an organization implies that IT projects should comply with the architecture roadmap. If that's not the case, then there must be a good reason for it.

To determine whether this is the case, an Architecture Compliance strategy should be adopted with specific measures to ensure compliance with the architecture. The Architecture Capability Framework includes a set of processes, guidelines, and a checklist for ensuring project compliance to the architecture, including:

- Project Impact Assessments that illustrate how the enterprise architecture impacts on the major projects within an organization
- The Architecture Compliance Review process (see Figure 24), which is a formal process for reviewing the compliance of projects to the enterprise architecture

8.5 Architecture Skills Framework

The Architecture Capability Framework provides a set of role, skill, and experience norms for staff undertaking enterprise architecture work.

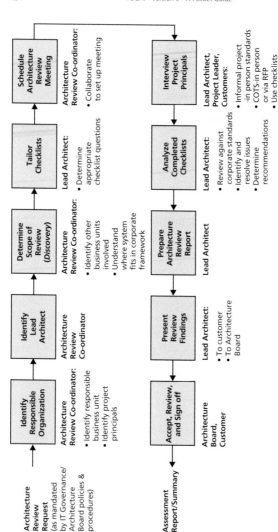

Figure 24: Architecture Compliance Review Process

"Enterprise Architecture" and "Enterprise Architect" are widely used but poorly defined terms in the IT industry today. They are used to denote a variety of practices and skills applied in a wide variety of architecture domains. There is a need for better classification to enable more implicit understanding of what type of architect/architecture is being described.

This lack of uniformity leads to difficulties for organizations seeking to recruit or assign/promote staff to fill positions in the architecture field. Because of the different usages of terms, there is often misunderstanding and miscommunication between those seeking to recruit for, and those seeking to fill, the various roles of the architect.

The TOGAF Architecture Skills Framework attempts to address this need by providing definitions of the architecting skills and proficiency levels required of personnel, internal or external, who are to perform the various architecting roles defined within the TOGAF framework.

Skill categories include:
- Generic Skills, typically comprising leadership, team-working, inter-personal skills, etc.
- Business Skills & Methods, typically comprising business cases, business process, strategic planning, etc.
- Enterprise Architecture Skills, typically comprising modeling, building block design, applications and role design, systems integration, etc.
- Program or Project Management Skills, typically comprising managing business change, project management methods and tools, etc.
- IT General Knowledge Skills, typically comprising brokering applications, asset management, migration planning, SLAs, etc.
- Technical IT Skills, typically comprising software engineering, security, data interchange, data management, etc.
- Legal Environment, typically comprising data protection laws, contract law, procurement law, fraud, etc.

Appendix A Migration Summary

A.1 Introduction

This appendix contains high-level migration information – a summary description of what is changed from TOGAF 8.1.1. Readers are assumed to be familiar with the content of TOGAF 8.1.1.

	TOGAF 9 Chapter	Derivation from TOGAF 8.1.1
	Part I: Introduction	
1	Introduction	Material revised; based on Chapter 1 This revised chapter describes the structure and provides an executive overview of enterprise architecture and the benefits of using TOGAF. Some of the previous contents have been moved to the new Chapters 2 and 4.
2	Core Concepts	New chapter This new chapter introduces the core concepts of TOGAF; what it is; what is architecture in the context of TOGAF; what types of architecture does TOGAF deal with; the ADM. It introduces key concepts such as deliverables, artifacts, and building blocks. It introduces the Enterprise Continuum and the Architecture Repository. It introduces the establishment and operations of an Enterprise Architecture Capability. It describes considerations for using TOGAF with other frameworks. It also contains the TOGAF Document Categorization Model which is used to structure release management of the specification itself.
3	Definitions	Derived from Chapter 36, reworked into formal definitions & abbreviations This revised chapter contains the key terms and definitions. Other supplementary definitions and abbreviations have been moved to separate appendices.

	TOGAF 9 Chapter	Derivation from TOGAF 8.1.1
4	Release Notes	New chapter This is a new chapter containing information on this release of the document. It contains an overview of what's new, the benefits of the changes, and summary mappings of the structure of the document from TOGAF 8.1.1 to TOGAF 9 and *vice versa*. It also includes information on terms and conditions for using TOGAF and where to download it.
Part II: Architecture Development Method		
5	Introduction	Material revised; based on Chapter 3 The changes made in this chapter are to position the ADM with respect to the Architecture Repository, and to Part III: ADM Guidelines and Techniques. The concept of document versioning is introduced with an example.
6	Preliminary Phase	Material revised; based on Chapter 4 The Approach has been expanded considerably to address in addition the definition of the enterprise, key drivers and elements for the organization, requirements for architecture work, management frameworks and their relationship, as well as enterprise maturity. There are now explicit Steps defined, whereas previously there were none.
7	Phase A: Architecture Vision	Material revised; based on Chapter 5 Business Scenarios are now called out as a separate section in Approach; previously they were included as a subsection to Steps. The Steps have been revised to additionally include an evaluation of Business Capabilities, Readiness for Business Transformation, definition of Target Architecture Value Propositions and KPIs, and identification of Business Transformation Risks and Mitigation activities. The Inputs and Outputs are reorganized to match the deliverables for TOGAF 9.

	TOGAF 9 Chapter	Derivation from TOGAF 8.1.1
8	Phase B: Business Architecture	Material revised; based on Chapter 6 The Approach is revised to discuss the Architecture Repository rather than the Enterprise Continuum. The description of the Gap Analysis technique is moved to Part III: ADM Guidelines and Techniques. A revised sequence of Steps is introduced. This same sequence of steps is also used in Phases C and D. The Inputs and Outputs are reorganized to match the deliverables for TOGAF 9. A key difference is the introduction of two container documents: the Architecture Definition Document and the Architecture Requirements Specification.
9	Phase C: Information Systems Architectures	Material revised; based on Chapter 7 The Inputs and Outputs are reorganized to match the deliverables for TOGAF 9.
10	Phase C: Data Architecture	Material revised; based on Chapter 8 In Approach: the reference to Enterprise Continuum is replaced with the Architecture Repository. The section on Gap Analysis is removed. A section on Key Considerations for Data Architecture is added. A revised sequence of Steps is introduced. This same sequence is also used in Phases B, C (Application Architecture), and D. The Inputs and Outputs are reorganized to match the deliverables for TOGAF 9.
11	Phase C: Application Architecture	Material revised; based on Chapter 9 In Approach: the reference to Enterprise Continuum is replaced with the Architecture Repository. The section on Gap Analysis is removed. A revised sequence of Steps is introduced. This same sequence is also used in Phases B, C (Data Architecture), and D. The Inputs and Outputs are reorganized to match the deliverables for TOGAF 9.

	TOGAF 9 Chapter	Derivation from TOGAF 8.1.1
12	Phase D: Technology Architecture	Material revised; based on Chapter 10 In Approach: the reference to Enterprise Continuum is replaced with the Architecture Repository. The Steps have undergone a major reorganization, and now use the same sequence also used in Phases B and C. The Inputs and Outputs are reorganized to match the deliverables for TOGAF 9.
13	Phase E: Opportunities & Solutions	Material revised; based on Chapter 11 This phase has had a major revision to add extensive detail on an Approach and Steps to move from Target Architectures to implementation via a series of Transition Architectures. The Inputs and Outputs are reorganized to match the deliverables for TOGAF 9.
14	Phase F: Migration Planning	Material revised; based on Chapter 12 This phase has had a major revision to add extensive detail on an Approach and Steps to finalize the Implementation and Migration Plan for the Transition Architectures identified in Phase E. The Inputs and Outputs are reorganized to match the deliverables for TOGAF 9.
15	Phase G: Implementation Governance	Material revised; based on Chapter 13 The Objectives include rewording and additions to emphasize the governance aspect of the phase. The Approach has been updated to include Business Value Realization. The Steps have had a major revision to include confirmation of scope for deployment with development management, identification of deployment skills and resources, guidance development for solutions deployment, compliance reviews, implementation of operations, and a post-implementation review.

	TOGAF 9 Chapter	**Derivation from TOGAF 8.1.1**
16	Phase H: Architecture Change Management	Material revised; based on Chapter 14 The Objectives have been reworked and including maximizing business value. The Approach is expanded to additionally include monitoring of the business and capacity management. The Steps have had a major revision, and additionally include establishment of the value realization process, deployment of monitoring tools, management of risks, analysis for change, and development of change requirements to meet performance targets.
17	ADM Architecture Requirements Management	No material change; maps to Chapter 15 The Inputs and Outputs are reorganized to match the deliverables for TOGAF 9.
	Part III: ADM Guidelines and Techniques	
18	Introduction	New chapter This new part is provided to support application of the ADM.
19	Applying Iteration to the ADM	New chapter This chapter describes the concept of iteration and shows potential strategies for applying iterative concepts to the ADM.
20	Applying the ADM at Different Enterprise Levels	New chapter This chapter describes the different types of architecture engagement that may occur at different levels of the enterprise and how the ADM process can be focused to support them.
21	Security Architecture and the ADM	New chapter; derived from Security White Paper (W055) This chapter provides specific security considerations for each phase of the ADM.
22	Using TOGAF to Define & Govern SOAs	New chapter This chapter describes how the SOA style of architecture can be supported by TOGAF.

	TOGAF 9 Chapter	Derivation from TOGAF 8.1.1
23	Architecture Principles	No material change; maps to Chapter 29 A new example principle of Service Orientation to the Business Principles.
24	Stakeholder Management	New chapter This chapter describes the technique of stakeholder management, an important discipline for architecture practitioners.
25	Architecture Patterns	No material change; maps to Chapter 28
26	Business Scenarios	No material change; maps to Chapter 34
27	Gap Analysis	New chapter; derived from Gap Analysis This chapter is introduced to allow the technique to be referenced from the ADM phases, and therefore reduce duplication of text.
28	Migration Planning Techniques	New chapter This chapter describes a number of techniques to support Phases E and F.
29	Interoperability Requirements	New chapter This chapter provides guidelines for developing interoperability requirements.
30	Business Transformation Readiness Assessment	New chapter This chapter describes a technique for identifying business transformation issues.
31	Risk Management	New chapter This chapter describes a technique for managing risk during an architecture or business transformation project.
32	Capability-Based Planning	New chapter This chapter describes the technique of capability-based planning.

	TOGAF 9 Chapter	Derivation from TOGAF 8.1.1
	Part IV: Architecture Content Framework	
33	Introduction	New chapter This new part of TOGAF addresses content output, providing a framework within which to place major work products.
34	Content Metamodel	New chapter This chapter provides a metamodel definition of all the types of building blocks within an architecture, showing how they can be described and how they relate to one another.
35	Architectural Artifacts	Derived from Chapter 31, plus new material This chapter is revised to address a set of atomic work products created when following the ADM. A diagram to illustrate the concepts from ISO/IEC 42010:2007 is introduced. Classes of viewpoints are defined: catalogs, matrices, and diagrams. Additional architecture viewpoints are added.
36	Architecture Deliverables	Revised from Chapter 16 A significant revision of the deliverables has been undertaken. A table is provided showing where deliverables are produced and consumed within the ADM cycle. A key difference is the introduction of two container documents: the Architecture Definition Document and the Architecture Requirements Specification.
37	Building Blocks	Revised from Chapter 32 The description of the building blocks specification process in the ADM has been updated to match the changes to the ADM steps. The section on Levels of Modeling has been removed.

	TOGAF 9 Chapter	Derivation from TOGAF 8.1.1
	Part V: Enterprise Continuum and Tools	
38	Introduction	New chapter
39	Enterprise Continuum	Derived from Chapters 17 and 18
		The explanation of the Enterprise Continuum has been rewritten to better explain its purpose and context, including its relationship to enterprise repositories.
		Organization Architectures has been updated to Organization-Specific Architectures in the diagram of the Architecture Continuum.
		Organization Solutions has been updated to Organization-Specific Solutions in the diagram of the Solutions Continuum.
		In the description of the Architecture Continuum, Enterprise Architectures is updated to Organization-Specific Architectures.
		In the description of the Solutions Continuum, Enterprise Solutions is updated to Organization-Specific Solutions.
40	Architecture Partitioning	New chapter
		This chapter describes the various characteristics that can be applied to classify and then partition architectures.
41	Architecture Repository	New chapter
		This chapter describes how the abstract classifications of architecture can be applied to a repository structure.
42	Tools for Architecture Development	No material change; maps to Chapter 38
		A reference has been added to the TOGAF certification program.
	Part VI: TOGAF Reference Models	
43	Foundation Architecture: Technical Reference Model	No material change; maps to Chapters 19 and 20
		The Detailed Platform Taxonomy is now a section of this chapter rather than being a separate chapter.

	TOGAF 9 Chapter	**Derivation from TOGAF 8.1.1**
44	Integrated Information Infrastructure Reference Model	No material change; maps to Chapter 22
	Part VII: Architecture Capability Framework	
45	Introduction	New chapter
46	Establishing an Architecture Capability	New chapter This chapter describes how to use the ADM to establish an architecture practice within an organization.
47	Architecture Board	Minimal change; maps to Chapter 23 Changes have been limited to minor editorial updates.
48	Architecture Compliance	Minimal change; maps to Chapter 24 The section Project Impact Assessments (Project Slices) has been removed.
49	Architecture Contracts	Minimal change; maps to Chapter 25 Wording is added to tie this chapter more closely to Architecture Governance. Instead of listing the contents of the Statement of Architecture Work, a reference to the definition in Part IV: Architecture Content Framework is added.
50	Architecture Governance	Minimal change, maps to Chapter 26 A reference to the TOGAF/COBIT mapping paper from ITGI is added. Some editorial rewording has been applied to the section Architecture Governance in Practice.
51	Architecture Maturity Models	Minimal change; maps to Chapter 27 Minor changes have been applied to refer to the latest version of ACMM.
52	Architecture Skills Framework	Some cosmetic changes; maps to Chapter 30 References to IT Architect have been replaced with Enterprise Architect.

	TOGAF 9 Chapter	Derivation from TOGAF 8.1.1
	Appendices	
A	Glossary of Supplementary Definitions	Derived from Chapter 36 The terms and definitions provided here have been split out from the original glossary as they are not specific to TOGAF.
B	Abbreviations	Derived from Chapter 36 This section has been split out from the original glossary.

Glossary

Application Architecture

A description of the major logical grouping of capabilities that manage the data objects necessary to process the data and support the business.

Architecture

Architecture has two meanings depending upon its contextual usage:

1. A formal description of a system, or a detailed plan of the system at component level to guide its implementation
2. The structure of components, their inter-relationships, and the principles and guidelines governing their design and evolution over time

Architecture Building Block (ABB)

A constituent of the architecture model that describes a single aspect of the overall model.

Architecture Continuum

A part of the Enterprise Continuum. A repository of architectural elements with increasing detail and specialization. This Continuum begins with foundational definitions like reference models, core strategies, and basic building blocks. From there it spans to Industry Architectures and all the way to an organization's specific architecture.

Architecture Development Method (ADM)

The core of TOGAF. A step-by-step approach to develop and use an enterprise architecture.

Architecture Framework

A foundational structure, or set of structures, which can be used for developing a broad range of different architectures. It should contain a method for designing an information system in terms of a set of building blocks, and for showing how the building blocks fit together. It should contain a set of tools and provide a common vocabulary. It should also include a list of recommended standards and compliant products that can be used to implement the building blocks.

Baseline Architecture
The existing defined system architecture before entering a cycle of architecture review and redesign.

Business Architecture
The business strategy, governance, organization, and key business processes information, as well as the interaction between these concepts.

Capability
An ability that an organization, person, or system possesses. Capabilities are typically expressed in general and high-level terms and typically require a combination of organization, people, processes, and technology to achieve. For example, marketing, customer contact, or outbound telemarketing.

Capability Architecture
A highly detailed description of the architectural approach to realize a particular solution or solution aspect.

Capability Increment
The output from a business change initiative that delivers an increase in performance for a particular capability of the enterprise.

Data Architecture
The structure of an organization's logical and physical data assets and data management resources.

Enterprise

The highest level (typically) of description of an organization and typically covers all missions and functions. An enterprise will often span multiple organizations.

Enterprise Continuum

A categorization mechanism useful for classifying architecture and solution artifacts, both internal and external to the Architecture Repository, as they evolve from generic Foundation Architectures to Organization-Specific Architectures.

Foundation Architecture

An architecture of generic services and functions that provides a foundation on which more specific architectures and architectural components can be built. The TOGAF Foundation Architecture includes a Technical Reference Model (TRM).

Gap

A statement of difference between two states. Used in the context of gap analysis, where the difference between the Baseline and Target Architecture is identified.

Governance

The discipline of monitoring, managing, and steering a business (or IS/IT landscape) to deliver the business outcome required.

Metamodel

A model that describes how and with what the architecture will be described in a structured way.

Repository

A system that manages all of the data of an enterprise, including data and process models and other enterprise information. Hence, the data in a repository is much more extensive than that in a data dictionary, which generally defines only the data making up a database.

Requirement

A quantitative statement of business need that must be met by a particular architecture or work package.

Risk Management

The management of risks and issues that may threaten the success of the enterprise architecture practice and its ability to meet is vision, goals, and objectives, and, importantly, its service provision.

Segment Architecture

A detailed, formal description of areas within an enterprise, used at the program or portfolio level to organize and align change activity.

Service Orientation

A way of thinking in terms of services and service-based development and the outcomes of services.

Service Oriented Architecture (SOA)

An architectural style that supports service orientation. It has the following distinctive features:

- It is based on the design of the services - which mirror real-world business activities - comprising the enterprise (or inter-enterprise) business processes.
- Service representation utilizes business descriptions to provide context (i.e., business process, goal, rule, policy, service interface, and service component) and implements services using service orchestration.

- It places unique requirements on the infrastructure - it is recommended that implementations use open standards to realize interoperability and location transparency.
- Implementations are environment-specific - they are constrained or enabled by context and must be described within that context.
- It requires strong governance of service representation and implementation.
- It requires a "Litmus Test", which determines a "good service".

Solution Architecture

A description of a discrete and focused business operation or activity and how IS/IT supports that operation. A Solution Architecture typically applies to a single project or project release, assisting in the translation of requirements into a solution vision, high-level business and/or IT system specifications, and a portfolio of implementation tasks.

Solution Building Block (SBB)

A candidate physical solution for an Architecture Building Block (ABB); e.g., a Commercial Off-The-Shelf (COTS) package, that is a component of the Acquirer view of the architecture.

Solutions Continuum

A part of the Enterprise Continuum. A repository of re-usable solutions for future implementation efforts. It contains implementations of the corresponding definitions in the Architecture Continuum.

Stakeholder

An individual, team, or organization (or classes thereof) with interests in, or concerns relative to, the outcome of the architecture. Different stakeholders with different roles will have different concerns.

Target Architecture

The description of a future state of the architecture being developed for an organization. There may be several future states developed as a roadmap to show the evolution of the architecture to a target state.

Technical Reference Model (TRM)

A structure which allows the components of an information system to be described in a consistent manner.

Technology Architecture

The logical software and hardware capabilities that are required to support deployment of business, data, and application services. This includes IT infrastructure, middleware, networks, communications, processing, and standards.

Transition Architecture

A formal description of the enterprise architecture showing periods of transition and development for particular parts of the enterprise. Transition Architectures are used to provide an overview of current and target capability and allow for individual work packages and projects to be grouped into managed portfolios and programs.

View

The representation of a related set of concerns. A view is what is seen from a viewpoint. An architecture view may be represented by a model to demonstrate to stakeholders their areas of interest in the architecture. A view does not have to be visual or graphical in nature.

Viewpoint

A definition of the perspective from which a view is taken. It is a specification of the conventions for constructing and using a view (often by means of an appropriate schema or template). A view is what you see; a viewpoint is where you are looking from – the vantage point or perspective that determines what you see.

Work Package

A set of actions identified to achieve one or more objectives for the business. A work package can be a part of a project, a complete project, or a program.